First World War
and Army of Occupation
War Diary
France, Belgium and Germany

60 DIVISION
Headquarters, Branches and Services
Royal Army Medical Corps
Assistant Director Medical Services
22 June 1916 - 30 November 1916

WO95/3026/8

The Naval & Military Press Ltd
www.nmarchive.com
Published in association with The National Archives

Published by

The Naval & Military Press Ltd

Unit 10 Ridgewood Industrial Park,

Uckfield, East Sussex,

TN22 5QE England

Tel: +44 (0) 1825 749494

www.naval-military-press.com

www.nmarchive.com

This diary has been reprinted in facsimile from the original. Any imperfections are inevitably reproduced and the quality may fall short of modern type and cartographic standards.

© Crown Copyright
Images reproduced by permission of The National Archives, London, England, 2015.

Contents

Document type	Place/Title	Date From	Date To
Heading	WO95/3026/8		
Heading	War Diary of A.D.M.S 60th (London) Division From June 22nd 1916 To July 31st 1916 Volume 1		
War Diary	Havre	22/06/1916	24/06/1916
War Diary	Flers	25/06/1916	27/06/1916
War Diary	Villers Chatel	28/06/1916	13/07/1916
War Diary	Hermaville	14/07/1916	31/07/1916
Operation(al) Order(s)	R.A.M.C. Operation Order No.1 By Colonel E.B. Dowsett, A.M.S. A.D.M.S. 60th (London) Division	11/07/1916	11/07/1916
Miscellaneous			
Operation(al) Order(s)	R.A.M.C. Operation Order No.2 By Colonel E.B. Dowsett, A.M.S. A.D.M.S. 60th (London) Division	12/07/1916	12/07/1916
Map	Scheme For Evacuating Sick And Wounded From 60th Divisional Area (Provisional)		
Map	Map		
Miscellaneous	Scheme Of Evacuating Sick 6 Wounded From 60th Divisional Area (Provisional)	23/07/1916	23/07/1916
Heading	War Diary of A.D.M.S 60th (London) Division From August 1st 1916 To August 31st 1916 Vol 3		
War Diary	Hermaville	01/08/1916	31/08/1916
Miscellaneous	Medical Arrangements for Scheme of Defence of Reserve Line	18/08/1916	18/08/1916
Miscellaneous	Medical Arrangements in the Event of A General Attack by The Enemy	25/08/1916	25/08/1916
Heading	War Diary (Medical) Of 60th (London) Division From Sept 1-16 To Sept 30-16 Volume 4		
War Diary	Hermaville	01/09/1916	30/09/1916
Heading	War Diary (Medical) Of A.D.M.S 60th (London) Division From 1st October 1916 To 31 October 1916 Volume 5		
War Diary	Hermaville	01/10/1916	25/10/1916
War Diary	Houvin Houvigneul	26/10/1916	27/10/1916
War Diary	Frhen Le Grand	28/10/1916	28/10/1916
War Diary	Bernaville	29/10/1916	31/10/1916
Miscellaneous	Scheme Of Medical Arrangements During Operations On Front From A.4.d.2.2 To A.4.a.5.2 (Approximately)		
Operation(al) Order(s)	R.A.M.C. Operation Order No.3	20/10/1916	20/10/1916
Operation(al) Order(s)	60th Division R.A.M.C. Operation Order No.4	22/10/1916	22/10/1916
Miscellaneous	Relief Table Of Field Ambulances Of 60th (London) Division		
Miscellaneous	Table "D"		
Miscellaneous	Field Ambulance Stores	22/10/1916	22/10/1916
Miscellaneous	Medical Officer 2/ Battn. London Regiment	22/10/1916	22/10/1916
Heading	War Diary (Medical) Of The D.M.S 60th (London) Division Volume From 1st November 16 To 30th November 16		
War Diary	Bernaville	01/11/1916	03/11/1916
War Diary	Ailly Le Haut Clocher	03/11/1916	30/11/1916
Operation(al) Order(s)	60th Division R.A.M.C. Operation Order No.5	02/11/1916	02/11/1916
Operation(al) Order(s)	60th Division R.A.M.C. Operation Order No.6	13/11/1916	13/11/1916

WO 95/3026/8

Medical

Confidential

War Diary
of D.D.M.S.
60th (London) Division.

From: June 22nd 1916 to July 31st 1916.

Volume 1

[signature] Colonel
D.D.M.S. 60th Division.

COMMITTEE FOR THE
MEDICAL HISTORY OF THE WAR
Date 13 SEP. '15

MEDICAL.

WAR DIARY OF A.D.M.S. 60th (LONDON) DIVISION. Army Form C. 2118.

INTELLIGENCE SUMMARY.
(Erase heading not required.)

I.

Instructions regarding War Diaries and Intelligence Summaries are contained in F. S. Regs., Part II. and the Staff Manual respectively. Title pages will be prepared in manuscript.

Place	Date	Hour	Summary of Events and Information	Remarks and references to Appendices
HAVRE	22.6.16	3.40 p.m.	left SOUTHAMPTON at 8.0 p.m. by S.S. PANCRAS	
	23.6.16	7.0 a.m.	Arrived at HAVRE. Disembarked at 10.0 a.m. Reported arrival to M.L.O.	C.h.7.
		2.30 p.m.	Proceeded to REST CAMP	C.h.7.
	24.6.16	3.30 p.m.	Entrained at POINT TROIS, HAVRE.	C.h.7.
FLERS	25.6.16	10.30 a.m.	Arrived at St POL - Proceeded to FLERS - H.Q. of 60th (London) DIVISION.	
		2.0 p.m.	Opened Office. 2/4 London Field Ambulance arrived at MAIZIERES. 2/5 Field Ambulance at PENIN	C.h.7
	26.6.16	10.0 a.m.	Reported to DDMS XVII Corps at AUBIGNY.	
			Proceeded to HERMAVILLE to see A.D.M.S. 51st Division and received information	
		4.30 p.m.	with regard to Places occupied by units of 51st Division and medical arrangements.	C.h.7
	27.6.16	9.0 a.m.	with ADMS 37th Division to Field Ambulances of that Division to inspect medical arrangements.	
			ORDERS received from DDMS GHQ for Capt. G.H.L.WHALE to report to No 13 General Hospital	
			2/1st London Field Ambulance arrived in billets at NEUVILLE AU CORNET.	
			ORDERS received for 1 Officer, 1 NCO and 6 men from each Field Ambulance	
			to be detailed for duty at various C.C.Ss.	
			Sanitary Section 60th London Division reported arrival at FLERS.	
		2.0 p.m.	Conference at D.D.M.S. Office AUBIGNY.	C.h.7

1577 Wt.W10791/1773 500,000 1/15 D. D. & L. A.D.S.S./Forms/C. 2118.

Army Form C. 2118.

WAR DIARY
INTELLIGENCE SUMMARY.
(Erase heading not required.)

Instructions regarding War Diaries and Intelligence Summaries are contained in F. S. Regs., Part II. and the Staff Manual respectively. Title pages will be prepared in manuscript.

Place	Date	Hour	Summary of Events and Information	Remarks and references to Appendices
VILLERS CHATEL	28.6.16	9.30 am	Left FLERS –	
		12.0 noon	Arrived at VILLERS CHATEL – Opened Office – 60th Division H.Q. established at VILLERS CHATEL. Sanitary Section billeted annexe VILLERS CHATEL. 2/6 London Field Ambulance moved to GUESTREVILLE	
		3.0 pm	To MATIGRES to inspect arrangements of 2/4 London Field Ambulance. To PENIN to inspect arrangements of 2/5 London Field Ambulance. To MINGOVAL to inspect place in view of probable move of 2/6 London Field Ambulance thither	
	29.6.16	9.30 am	To AUBIGNY to see DDMS XVII Corps – Then on to HERMAVILLE to see ADMS 51st Division and instructions to further inspect medical arrangements and positions in 51st Division Area	
		4.30 pm	At billets in VILLERS CHATEL inspected – Sanitary arrangements generally satisfactory but improvement needed – Water supplies inspected and notices posted and orders issued that all water must either be boiled or chlorinated before use.	
	30.6.16	9.30 am	To ADMS 51st Division at HERMAVILLE – Then to TINQUES to inspect Billets and to 2/5 Ambulance at PENIN to inspect medical arrangements – To TINCQUETTES to inspect Huts and accommodation there –	

1577 Wt.W10791/1773 500,000 1/15 D. D. & L.   A.D.S.S./Forms/C. 2118.

Army Form C. 2118.

WAR DIARY

INTELLIGENCE SUMMARY.
(Erase heading not required.)

Instructions regarding War Diaries and Intelligence Summaries are contained in F. S. Regs., Part II. and the Staff Manual respectively. Title pages will be prepared in manuscript.

Place	Date	Hour	Summary of Events and Information	Remarks and references to Appendices
VILLERS CHATEL	30.6.16	3.0 pm	To ECOIVRES to view medical arrangements – 15 ACQ to see Camp site.	C in J
	1.7.16	9.0 am	To MAIZIERES to inspect its medical arrangements of 2/4 London Field Ambulance. To GUESTREVILLE to inspect 2/6 London Field Ambulance which move to-day to MINGOVAL –	
		5.0 pm	To AUBIGNY to see DDMS XVII Corps.	
	2.7.16	9.30 a.m.	2/5 London Field Ambulance moved from PENIN to TINCQUETTE. To ACQ and to HAUTE AVESNES to view Field Ambulance Hutments.	C in J
		2.30 p.m.	To AUBIGNY to see DDMS XVII Corps. To inspect medical arrangements of 1/4 Field Ambulance at MINGOVAL. 2/4 London Field Ambulance moved from MAIZIERES to ACQ. Inspection of kitchen at VILLERS CHATEL by AA & QMG and DADMS.	C in J
	3.7.16	9.30 am	To TINCQUETTE to inspect medical arrangements of 2/5 London Field Ambulance. Baths opened at CAMBLIGNEUL under 1 Officer and 4 men of 2/6 London Field Ambulance.	
		2.30 pm	Baths at CAMBLIGNEUL inspected – To MINGOVAL to inspect arrangements of 2/6 London Field Ambulance.	C in J

WAR DIARY
INTELLIGENCE SUMMARY.

Army Form C. 2118.

Place	Date	Hour	Summary of Events and Information	Remarks and references to Appendices
VILLERS CHATEL	4.7.16	9.0 a.m	To ACQ to inspect accommodation & medical arrangements of 1/1st London Field Ambulance	C.u.d
		2.0 p.m	To HERMAVILLE to see ADMS 57th Division	C.u.d
	5.7.16	10.a.m	To AUBIGNY – Conference at DDMS Office. To inspect medical arrangements of 2/6 London Field Ambulance at MINGOVAL	
		2–3.0 p.m	To CAMBLIGNEUL to inspect billets. To DDMS office AUBIGNY	C.u.d
	6.7.16	2.30 p.m	To ADMS office 57th Divn at HERMAVILLE. To inspect medical arrangements of 1/5 London Field Ambulance at TINCQUETTE. C.u.d	
	7.7.16	9.0 a.m	With DADMS 57th Division to inspect medical arrangements at ACQ – MAROEUIL	C.u.d
		5.0 p.m	and at AUX RIETZ and at ANZIN.	
	8.7.16	9.0 a.m	With ADMS 57th Division to view medical arrangements at MAROEUIL – ANZIN – NEUVILLE ST VAAST and AUX RIETZ.	C.u.d
	9.7.16	10.a.m	Inspection of billets – latrines and water supplies at VILLERS CHATEL	C.u.d
		2.0 p.m	Conference at H.Q. 60th Division	
	10.7.16	9.0 a.m	To see medical arrangements at ACQ – MAROEUIL – ANZIN – MAISON BLANCHE and ARIANE.	

Army Form C. 2118.

WAR DIARY
~~INTELLIGENCE SUMMARY~~
(Erase heading not required.)

Instructions regarding War Diaries and Intelligence Summaries are contained in F.S. Regs., Part II. and the Staff Manual respectively. Title pages will be prepared in manuscript.

Place	Date	Hour	Summary of Events and Information	Remarks and references to Appendices
VILLERS CHATEL	10/7/16	3.0. p.m.	To TINCQUETTE to inspect medical arrangements of 2/5 Field Ambulance.	
	11/7/16	9.30 a.m.	Capt L W HOWLETT reported for duty with 2/5 London Field Ambulance vice Capt H W Wade 15 Cheshires	
			W.E.T.M. & Q.M.G. 15 TINQUES - TINCQUETTE - CAMBLIGNEUL - MAIZIERES 15 Cheshires inspected general condition	
		2.0 p.m	Conference at D.D.M.S. office AUBIGNY.	
			60th Division R.A.M.C. OPERATION ORDERS No I issued	Appendix I
	12-7-16	10-0 a.m.	BATHING facilities inspected at MONTST ELOY - ACQ - MAROEUIL ETRUN ECOIVRES and HERMAVILLE -	
			Capt. FIELD HALL M.O. 2/22 Bau. London Regt for temporary duty of 2/6 London Field Ambulance - Capt. TANEYSMITH from 2/6 London Field Ambulance to be M.O. 2/22nd Batt. (temporary)	
			2/4 London Field Ambulance moved from ACQ to ECOIVRES	
			60th Division R.A.M.C OPERATION ORDERS No II issued	Appendix II
	13/7/16	10.0 a.m.	Took over administration of new area from ADMS 57th Division.	
			60th Division R.A.M.C ROUTINE ORDERS No 1-8 issued.	
		2.0 p.m	Visited ADS ANZIN and C.Ps at ARIANE and MADAGASCAR	

Army Form C. 2118.

Instructions regarding War Diaries and Intelligence Summaries are contained in F. S. Regs., Part II. and the Staff Manual respectively. Title pages will be prepared in manuscript.

WAR DIARY
~~INTELLIGENCE SUMMARY.~~
(Erase heading not required.)

VI.

Place	Date	Hour	Summary of Events and Information	Remarks and references to Appendices
VILLERS CHATEL	13.7.16		2/5 Londn Field Ambulance moves from TINCQUETTE to HAUTE AVESNES. 2/6 Londn Field Ambulance moves from MINGOVAL to HAUTE AVESNES.	C.h.d
HERMAVILLE	14.7.16	8.30 a.m.	Head Quarters 60th London Division moves from VILLERS CHATEL to HERMAVILLE	
		10.0 a.m.	DADMS 60th London Division with DADMS (Sanitation) III Army and DADMS XVII Corps inspected MAROEUIL – MONT ST ELOY – BOIS des ALEUX – BRAY – ETRUN AUX RIETZ and NEUVILLE ST VAAST	C.h.d
	15.7.16	10.0 a.m.	DADMS XVII Corps came to discuss the provision of Baths. Orders issued re Baths. Orders issued prohibiting use of water for drinking purposes unless previously boiled or chlorinated. 60th Division RAMC ROUTINE ORDERS No 9 – 11 issued M.D.S. at ECOIVRES and HAUTE AVESNES inspected. RAPs 179 Infantry Bgde and C.P. at POSTE CENTRALE inspected	(C.h.d)
	16.7.16	9.30 a.m.	Three RAPs h. & P. sectrs inspected and ADS at AUX RIETZ. DADMS inspected Catholic Sanitary Arrangements at HERMAVILLE – Additional Latrines to be provided – many latrines to be repaired. Billets require disinfection.	
		6 p.m.	Billets cleared – much refuse to be disposed of – Arrangements for necessary fatigues made.	C.h.d

1577 Wt.W10791/1773 500,000 1/15 D. D. & L. A.D.S.S./Forms/C. 2118.

Army Form C. 2118.

Instructions regarding War Diaries and Intelligence Summaries are contained in F. S. Regs., Part II. and the Staff Manual respectively. Title pages will be prepared in manuscript.

WAR DIARY
INTELLIGENCE SUMMARY.
(Erase heading not required.)

VII

Place	Date	Hour	Summary of Events and Information	Remarks and references to Appendices
HERMAVILLE	17.7.16	9.30 am	To TILLOY with reference to alleged outbreak there of Diphtheria - Reported to DDMS XVII Corps that no cases could be heard of. C.L.D.	
		2.30 pm	Baths at ETRUN and MAROEUIL inspected - Disinfecting Lorry at MAROEUIL inspected and working checked. 60th Division RAMC ROUTINE ORDERS nos 12 - 20 issued C.L.D.	
	18.7.16	10.0 am	DADMS with ADVS 60th Division to BAILLEUL re supposed Enteric cases.	
		2.0 pm	Conference at DDMS office AUBIGNY.	
		4.30 p.m.	To M.D.S. at ECOIVRES. 60th Division RAMC ROUTINE ORDERS nos 21 - 24 issued C.L.D.	
	19.7.16	9.30 am	With O.C. 9/b Field Ambulance to inspect MDS HAUTE AVESNES, ADS at ANZIN and C.Ps and RAPs in major Sect - MADAGASCAR and ROUTE de LILLE.	
		4.30 pm	DADMS to DDMS office AUBIGNY - Further inspection of HERMAVILLE made. C.L.D.	
	20.7.16	9.15 am	With DDMS XVII Corps to view medical arrangements at Scene of recent operations DADMS to DADMS XVII Corps at AUBIGNY re Dental cases. Inspected improvements now effected in general sanitary condition at HERMAVILLE C.L.D.	

Army Form C. 2118.

WAR DIARY
or
INTELLIGENCE SUMMARY.
(Erase heading not required.)

Instructions regarding War Diaries and Intelligence Summaries are contained in F. S. Regs., Part II. and the Staff Manual respectively. Title pages will be prepared in manuscript.

VIII

Place	Date	Hour	Summary of Events and Information	Remarks and references to Appendices
HERMAVILLE	21.7.16	9.0 am	AMBALA (A) CAVALRY FIELD AMBULANCE moved to ACQ. Inspected ADS at AUX RIETZ - C.P. at NEUVILLE ST VAAST - MDSs at ECOIVRES and at ACQ.	
		5-0 pm	To 60th Division Supply Column at TILLOY. 60th Division RAMC ROUTINE ORDERS Nos 25-28 Issued.	(In. ?)
	22.7.16	10 am to 6.0 pm	Inspected MDSs at HAUTE AVESNES and ECOIVRES - RAPs on right 17.9.15 Verge and C.P. at POSTE CENTRALE - Inspected Convalescen Camp & Grenade School at HERMAVILLE (DDMS)	(In. ?)
	23.7.16	10-30 am	Accompanied AA & QMG - 60th Division inspecting General Condition of HERMAVILLE	
		2.30 pm	Inspected MDSs at HAUTE AVESNES - ADS at ANZIN - and M.I.R. at MAROEUIL & (Provisional) area	Appendix III
			SCHEME of Evacuating Sick and wounded from 60th Divisional Area	(In. ?)
	24.7.16	9.30 am	With C.O.C. 60th Division to inspect MDS at ACQ - ECOIVRES - HAUTE AVESNES. 60th Division RAMC ROUTINE ORDERS No 29 - 31 Issued	(In. ?)
	25.7.16	9.30 am	DADMS with DADMS (Sanitation) III Army and DADMS XVII Corps Inspected General Sanitary Conditions and latrins at ACQ - and ECOIVRES.	
		2.0 pm	Conference at DDMS Office AUBIGNY.	(In. ?)

Army Form C. 2118.

WAR DIARY
or
INTELLIGENCE SUMMARY
(Erase heading not required.)

Instructions regarding War Diaries and Intelligence Summaries are contained in F. S. Regs., Part II. and the Staff Manual respectively. Title Pages will be prepared in manuscript.

Place	Date	Hour	Summary of Events and Information	Remarks and references to Appendices
HERMAVILLE	25.7.16	5.30 pm	To TILLOY to inspect Motor Ambulance Convoy with 13 Frances metal.	(M.J)
	26.7.16	10-0 am	With DDMS XVII Corps to MDSs at ACQ - ECOIVRES and HAUTE AVESNES.	
		12-0 noon	DADMS with AAQMG 60th Division made further inspection of HERMAVILLE billets Division RAMC Routine orders nos 32-35 issued	(M.J)
	27.7.16	9.15 am	Visited MDS at ECOIVRES - ADS at AUXRIETZ - C.P. at NEUVILLE ST VAAST and RAPs. Left 180th Bgde — Capt. C. BURROWS evacuated sick to No 42. C.C.S	(M.J)
	28.7.16	9.30 am	Visited ADS ANZIN - C.P. ROUTE de LILLE - RAPs left 181 Bgde - Old Artillery HQ	(M.J)
		5-0 pm	on MADAGASCAR inspected with a view to establishing a further ADS in this area if necessary	(M.J)
	29.7.16	9.15 am	With DMS 3rd Army and DDMS XVII Corps to inspect MDSS an ACQ - ECOIVRES and HAUTE AVESNES.	(M.J)
		2-0 pm	60th Divisional RAMC Routine Orders Nos 36-39 issued.	(M.J)
	30.7.16	9.30	Visited Central Group Artillery - RAPs Dug-outs - Kitchens inspected. On to see M.O	
		to	2/13 Bn in MAISON BLANCHE and to M.O. 7/16 - N sector to arrange plans for new	
		4-30 pm	dug outs and medical arrangements.	(M.J)
	31.7.16	10-0 am	To O.C. Artillery HQ at MADAGASCAR to further arrange particulars of to bring west - Q. to C.P. at ARIANE & MADAGASCAR and ADS ANZIN	(M.J)

E. Boutell
COLONEL
ASSISTANT DIRECTOR OF MEDICAL SERVICES
60TH (LONDON) DIVISION.

SECRET.　　　　　　　　　　　　　　　　　　　　　　　Copy No 6

R.A.M.C. Operation Order No. 1.
by
Colonel E.B. Dowsett, A.M.S.
A.D.M.S. 60th (London) Division.

Ref. Maps Sheet 11 LENS - 1 - 100,000.
　　　　　　Sheet 36^B FRANCE - 1 - 40,000
　　　　　　Sheet 36^C　　"　　　　"
　　　　　　Sheet 51^B　　"　　　　"
　　　　　　Sheet 51^C　　"　　　　"

Appendix 1.

11th July 1916.

Information.

1. The 60th (London) Division will take over the front at present held by the 51st (Highland) Division between 11th and 17th July, 1916.

2. The Command of the Front will be taken over by G.O.C., 60th Division at 10 am, 14th July, 1916.

3. A.D.M.S. 60th Division assumes responsibility for evacuation from the front from 10 am, 13th July, 1916.

Orders.

4. Reliefs of Field Ambulances will be carried out according to attached table.

5. March Table of Main bodies will be notified later.

6. Receipts will be given by Os.C. Field Ambulances for any stores, including Red X Stores, handed over by Os.C. Field Ambulances, 51st Division. Receipts will be obtained for any stores handed over by Os.C. Field Amboes. 60th Division to Os.C. Field Ambulances, 51st Division

7. Patients left in Field Ambulance Stations by 51st Divn. will be shown as Transfers in A & D Books, with original numbers, and nominal rolls with all necessary particulars will be obtained by Os.C. respective Field Ambulances.

8. Details to be arranged by Os.C. concerned.

9. Sections at present under instruction in various Field Ambulances of 51st Division will return to their respective Units at their <u>new</u> areas on afternoon of Thursday 13th July, 1916.

10. The Sanitary Section will move to HERMAVILLE on ~~Thursday 13th,~~ *Friday 14th July* 1916, and take up billets allotted them by Camp Commandant, who will notify time of march.

11. Further orders will be issued re details of evacuation from front.

Refilling Points on Arrival in New Area.

12. 2/4th London Field Ambulance　　　　　　　ACQ

　　　2/5th London Field Ambulance)
　　　2/6th London Field Ambulance)　　　　HAUTE AVESNES.

13. Mobile Veterinary Section will be established on 15th July, 1916 on ARRAS - ST.POL road ½ mile S. of AUBIGNY.

Reports.

14. 60th Divl. Hqrs. open at HERMAVILLE at 10 am 14 July 1916

15. Acknowledge.

Copy 1. H.Q. ("G") of 60th Divn.
　　　2. 2/4th London Field Ambulance
　　　3. 2/5th London Field Ambulance
　　　4. 2/6th London Field Ambulance
　　　5. Sanitary Section
　　　6. War Diary
　　　7. File.　　　Copy No. 8. D.D.M.S. XVII Corps.

E.B. Dowsett
COLONEL
ASSISTANT DIRECTOR OF
MEDICAL SERVICES
60TH (LONDON) DIVISION.

DATE	UNIT	FROM	TO	RELIEVES	PROCEEDING TO
July 12th	Advanced Party 2/4th London Field Ambce.	ACQ	ECOIVRES	Advanced Party 1/2nd (High.) Field Ambce.	ACQ.
"	Advanced Party 2/5th London Field Ambce.	TINCQUETTE	HAUTE AVESNES	Advanced Party 1/3rd (High.) Field Ambce.	TINCQUETTE
"	Advanced Party 2/6th London Field Ambce.	MINGOVAL	HAUTE AVESNES	Advanced Party 2/1st (High.) Field Ambce.	MINGOVAL
Night 12/13th	Adv. Dressing Stn. Party. 2/4th London Field Ambce.	ACQ	AUX RIETZ.	Adv. Dressing Stn. Party 1/2nd (High.) Field Ambce.	ECOIVRES.
"	Adv. Dressing Stn. Party. 2/6th London Field Ambce.	MINGOVAL	ANZIN ST. AUBIN	Adv. Dressing Stn. Party 2/1st (High.) Field Ambce.	HAUTE AVESNES
13th	2/4th London Field Ambce.	ACQ	ECOIVRES	1/2nd (High.) Field Ambce.	ACQ
"	2/5th London Field Ambce.	TINCQUETTE	HAUTE AVESNES	1/3rd (High.) Field Ambce. Divisional Rest station.	TINCQUETTE
"	2/6th London Field Ambce.	MINGOVAL	HAUTE AVESNES	1/2nd (High.) Field Ambce.	MINGOVAL.

SECRET   Copy No. 5

R.A.M.C. OPERATION ORDER NO. 2.
by
Colonel E.B. Dowsett, A.M.S.
A.D.M.S. 60th (London) Division.

APPENDIX II.

Ref Map. Sheet 11   LENS - 1 in 100,000
"   36^B FRANCE - 1 in 40,000
"   36^C FRANCE   "   "
"   51^B FRANCE   "   "
"   51^C FRANCE   "   "
Secret Trench Map No. 83. 84. 85.

Information. 1. Regimental Aid Posts are situated approximately at the following places:-
      (a) S.27. d. 3. 8.
      (b) S.27. a. 7. 5.
      (c) A. 3. b. 1. 1. Portugue
      (d) A.10. a. 1. 5.
      (e) A.15. a.10. 5.
      (f) A.15. b. 1. 2.
      (g) A.28. b. 4. 6. LA SABLIERE
      (h) A.21. b. 8. 9. POSTE LILLE
      (j) A.27. a. 5. 4.

(a),(b) & (c) are in Left Sector

(d),(e) & (f) are in Centre Sector.

(g),(h) & (j) are in Right Sector.

Orders
(On arrival in new area on 13-7-16)

2. The 2/4th London Field Ambulance will collect and evacuate sick and wounded from all R.A.Ps. in Left & Centre Sectors.

Collecting Posts for relays of bearers are as follows:-

(a) For Left Sector   -   NEUVILLE ST. VAAST (A.8.b.6.8.)

(b) For Centre Sector -   POSTE CENTRALE (A.9.c.1.15.)

Adv. Dressing Station for this area is at AUX RIETZ (A.8.c.5.7.)

Evacuation from AUX RIETZ to 2/4th London Field Ambce. Main Dressing Station at ECOIVRES is by Motor Ambulance at Night and by TERRITORIAL AVENUE by day. In cases of extreme urgency only, and if conditions permit, may the car be used from AUX RIETZ by day.

3. The 2/6th London Field Ambulance will collect and evacuate sick and wounded from all R.A.Ps. in Right Sector.

Collecting Posts for Relays of Bearers are as follows:-

(a) For Northern Half of Sector - BETHUNE-ARRAS Road at
    A.20.d.5.7.

(b) For Southern Half of Sector - On LILLE-ARRAS Road at
    A.28.c.1.1.
    MADAGASCAR at A.26.d.9.4.

Adv. Dressing Station for this area is at ANZIN ST. AUBIN, G.7.b.8.8. Evacuations from Collecting Posts is by hand carriage or wheeled stretcher by day, and by motor Ambulance Car by night by BETHUNE Road and LILLE Road, via ST. CATHERINE Road.

Evacuations from ANZIN ST. AUBIN is by Car by day or night to 2/6th London Field Ambulance Main Dressing Station at HAUTE AVESNES.

4. The 2/5th London Field Ambulance will form Divisional Rest Station at HAUTE AVESNES.

5. The 2/4th and 2/6th London Field Ambulances will send up 4 bearers to remain at each of the R.A.Ps. from which they are evacuating. These bearers will be relieved every 48 hours from the respective Adv. Dressing Stations.

6. The 2/4th and 2/6th London Field Ambulances will each send to the other R.A.Ps. as requested by the M.Os. of Artillery Groups, and other Units not in the Line.

H.Q. 60th Division.
July 12th 1916.   A.D.M.S. 60th (London) Division.   Colonel.

Copy No. 1. D.D.M.S. XVll Corps.
         2 2/4th London Field Ambulance.
         3 2/5th London Field Ambulance.
         4 2/6th London Field Ambulance.
         5 War Diary
         6 File

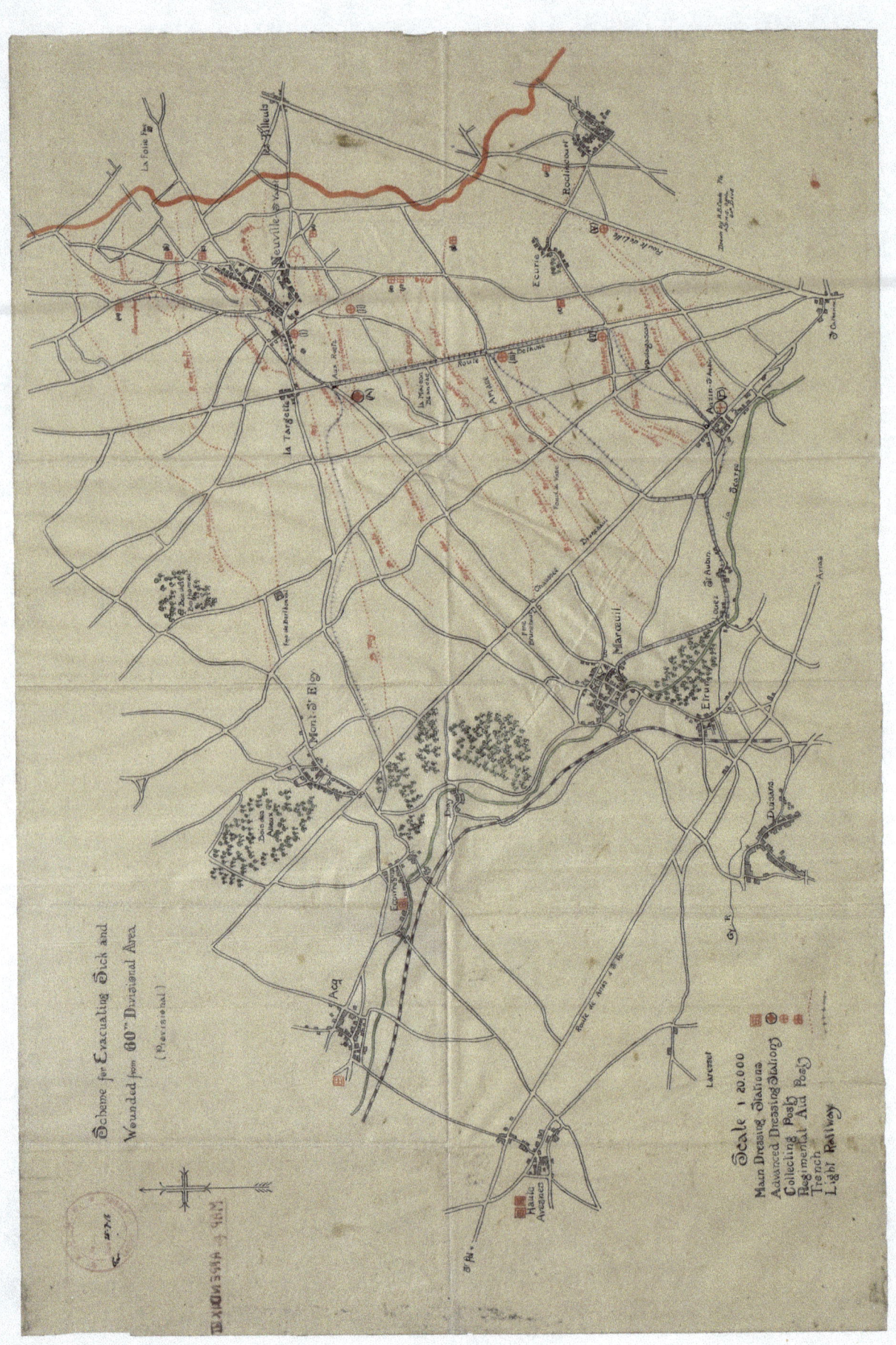

Scheme of Evacuating Sick & Wounded from 60th Divisional Area (Provisional).

APPENDIX III.

Ref. Maps. Sheet. 11 LENS, 1 in 100,000
" 36ᴮ FRANCE, 1 in 400,00
" 36ᶜ " " "
" 51ᴮ " " "
" 51ᶜ " " "

SITUATIONS. 1. <u>Regimental Aid Posts</u> are situated as follows:—

(a) S. 27. a. 7. 5. }
(b) S. 27. d. 3. 8. } 180th Infantry Brigade.
(c) A. 3. b. 1. 1. }
(d) A. 10. a. 1. 5. }
(e) A. 15. d. 10. 5. } 179th Infantry Brigade.
(f) A. 15. b. 1. 2. }
(g) A. 21. b. 8. 9. }
(h) A. 27. a. 5. 4. } 181st Infantry Brigade.
(j) A. 28. b. 4. 6. }

Three convenient Aid Posts are also being formed for the 3 groups of Artillery, each group under one Medical Officer.

2. <u>Collecting Posts</u> for Relays of Field Ambulance bearers are situated as follows:—

	ACCOMMODATION
	LYING / SITTING
(i) A. 8. b. 6. 8. (NEUVILLE ST. VAAST) for bearers evacuating from (a) (b) & (c)	60 / 180
(ii) A. 9. c. 1. 5. (POSTE CENTRALE) for bearers evacuating from (d) (e) & (f)	35 / 105
(iii) A. 20. d. 6. 4. (ARIANE) for bearers evacuating from (g)	10 / 40
(iv) A. 26. d. 9. 4. (MADAGASCAR) for bearers evacuating from (h) & ARIANE	12 / 30
(v) A. 28. c. 1. 1. (ROUTE DE LILLE) for bearers evacuating from (j)	45 / 100

3. <u>Advanced Dressing Stations</u> are situated as follows:—

	ACCOMMODATION
	LYING / SITTING
(A) A. 8. c. 5. 5. (AUX RIETZ) - 2/4th Lond. Fd. Amb.	70 / 210
(B) G. 7. b. 8. 8. (ANZIN ST. AUBIN) - 2/6th Lond. Fd. Amb.	30 / 100

4. <u>Main Dressing Stations</u> are situated as follows:—

ECOIVRES — 2/4th Lond. Field Amb.
HAUTE AVESNES — 2/6th Lond. Field Amb.
ACQ. — AMBALLA (A) Field Amb.
(For reception of Native troops only).

MEANS OF EVACUATION.

1. <u>From R.A.P's.</u> casualties are evacuated:—

   By day — From all R.A.Ps. by hand carriage to Collecting Stations as above, except from (a) when the light railway can be used as far as N.E. corner of NEUVILLE ST. VAAST, when hand carriage is used.

   By night — From (a) (b) & (c) by hand carriage by shortest route to Light Railway and thence all the way by trolley to AUX RIETZ.

   Four Field Ambulance bearers are permanently kept at each R.A.P.

2. <u>From Field Ambulance Collecting Stations</u> casualties are evacuated:—

   By day — From all Collecting Posts by hand carriage to Advanced Dressing Station. Urgent cases by day are taken by wheeled stretcher carriage from ARIANE to ANZIN via MADAGASCAR.

   By night — From NEUVILLE ST VAAST to AUX RIETZ by Light Railway from ARIANE, MADAGASCAR & ROUTE DE LILLE to ANZIN ~~AUX RIETZ~~ by Motor Ambulance Car.

3. <u>From Adv. Dressing Stations</u> casualties are evacuated:—

   By day — From AUX RIETZ by hand carriage via TERRITORIAL TRENCH to MAROEUIL and thence by Motor Ambulance Car to Main Dressing Station at ECOIVRES.
   From ANZIN by Motor Ambulance Car to Main Dressing Station at HAUTE AVESNES.
   Very urgent cases by day by motor ambulance Car from AUX RIETZ to ECOIVRES via MAROEUIL.

   By night — From AUX RIETZ by Motor Ambulance Car to ECOIVRES via MONT ST. ELOY.
   From ANZIN as by day.

   All native troops of the 1st. Indian Cavalry Division are evacuated to Main Dressing Station at ACQ.

Evacuation from back area.

Arrangements have been made with all Units and portions of Units not in front line, i.e. Artillery, R.E., Pioneers, A.S.C. etc. for all sick & casualties to be sent to one or other Adv. Dressing Station.

Divisional Rest Station.

Formed by 2/5 London Field Ambulance at HAUTE AVESNES.

N.B. Many Improvements are in process of construction at both R.A.Ps, Adv. Dressing Stns, and Main Dressing Stations, and extra accommodation is already earmarked for any emergency.

23·9·16

COLONEL
ASSISTANT DIRECTOR OF
MEDICAL SERVICES
60TH (LONDON) DIVISION.

Confidential.

Aug. 1916.

Vol 3

War Diary
of
A.D.M.S. 60th (London) Division.
from
August 1st 1916. to August 31st 1916.

COMMITTEE FOR THE
MEDICAL HISTORY OF THE W...
Date -5 OCT 1915

Original.

Army Form C. 2118.

WAR DIARY
INTELLIGENCE SUMMARY.
(Erase heading not required.)

MEDICAL.

SHEET 1.

Place	Date	Hour	Summary of Events and Information	Remarks and references to Appendices
HERMAVILLE	Aug 1.	10.0 am	To inspect medical arrangements of 2/5 London Field Ambulance (D.R.S.) at HAUTE AVESNES.	
"	"	15	To inspect medical arrangements of 2/6 London Field Ambulance at HAUTE AVESNES.	
"	"	1 p.m	To inspect medical arrangements and accommodation of 2/4 London Field Ambulance at ECOIVRES. C.L.P	
"	Aug 2.	2.30 p.m.	Conference of O.C. and second in command of 2/4 - 2/5 and 2/6 London Field Ambulances at ADMS Office HERMAVILLE	
			R.A.M.C.-(60TH London Division) ROUTINE ORDERS 40-45 issued.	C.L.D
"	Aug 3	10. a.m	Investigated condition of advanced trench which runs parallel with GOODMAN TRENCH and into the BIRMINGHAM DUMP Trench line with a view to its being used for medical purposes.	C.L.D
"	Aug 4	11.0 a.m.	With G.S.O.I. 60TH Division to view and investigate practicality of opening up a trench near GOODMAN TRENCH.	
			Invalids A.D.S. AUX RIETZ - and to confer with G.O.C. 180TH Infantry Bde.	
"	Aug 5	10. a.m	With D.D.M.S XVII Corps and Col. GREY - Consulting Surgeon to IV ARMY to 2/4 London Field Ambulance at ECOIVRES and to 2/5 and 2/6 London Field Ambulance at HAUTE AVESNES	
		2.0 p.m	To ANZIN to meet G.O.C 60TH Division to see accommodation there at A.D.S. with a view to it being increased	

Army Form C. 2118.

SHEET II

WAR DIARY

INTELLIGENCE SUMMARY.

(Erase heading not required.)

Instructions regarding War Diaries and Intelligence Summaries are contained in F.S. Regs., Part II. and the Staff Manual respectively. Title pages will be prepared in manuscript.

Place	Date	Hour	Summary of Events and Information	Remarks and references to Appendices
HERMAVILLE	Aug 5	2.30pm	Board held at MAROUIL on P.B. Men - ADMS presided - Members Major FEGEN and Capt THORNTON - 2/b Field Ambulance	C.n.F.
"	Aug 6	11.0 am	DADMS with A.A. & Q.M.G. 60th Division to inspect Convalescent Camps - Crinade School and Reinforcement Billets at HERMAVILLE	
		2.30pm	ADMS C.R.E 60th Division to ANZIN to inspect proposed extension of A.D.S. Rear	
		6.0 pm	Conference at HERMAVILLE with O.s.C. 2/4 and 2/6 London Field Ambulances re medical arrangements for evacuation of wounded.	
			War Diaries forwarded to H.Q. BASE	C n F
"	Aug 7	11-0 am	Inspection of billets at Reinforcement Camp HERMAVILLE	
		5.30 pm	To ECOIVRES to interview O.C. 2/4 London Field Ambulance and to inspect accommodation	
			To HAUTE AVESNES to interview O.C. 2/5 & 2/6 London Field Ambulances and to inspect accommodation	
			Under orders of DDMS XVII Corps Capt KIMBER reported for temporary duty with 172 Tunnelling Coy R.E.	
			60th London Divisional R.A.M.C. ROUTINE orders no 46 - 50 issued.	
			H.Q. 60th Division instructed ADMS to act as ADMS XVII Corps from Aug 5 to Aug 11 inclusive	C n F

Army Form C. 2118.

WAR DIARY
INTELLIGENCE SUMMARY.
(Erase heading not required.)

SHEET III

Instructions regarding War Diaries and Intelligence Summaries are contained in F. S. Regs., Part II. and the Staff Manual respectively. Title pages will be prepared in manuscript.

Place	Date	Hour	Summary of Events and Information	Remarks and references to Appendices
HERMAVILLE	Aug 8	9.15am	To ECURIE – Inspection water supplies – Latrine accommodation and alteration to RAP	
		12.30 p.m	To inspect ADS at ANZIN	C.in.d
			DADMS XII Corps came to consult acting D.DMS XII Corps.	
"	Aug 9	10.am	To inspect ADS at AUX RIETZ and to further inspect trench near GOODMAN TRENCH and RAP at NEVILLE ST VAAST	C.in.d
"	Aug 10	2.30 pm	Visit of H.M. the KING and H.R.H. Prince of WALES to Divisional Area – ADMS accompanied the Divisional Staff to Mt. ST ELOY.	
		5.30 pm	To DDMS office AUBIGNY.	C.in.d
			60th Divisional ROUTINE ORDERS Nos. 51 – 54 issued	
"	Aug 11	10. am.	To DDMS office AUBIGNY.	
		2.30 p.m	Inspected Sanitary & Cooking arrangements of Right Artillery Group.	
		10. am	DADMS and OC Sanitary Section accompanied ADMS (Sanitation) III Army on tour of his portion of HERMAVILLE – HAUTE AVESNES – ECOIVRES and FRÉVIN CAPELLE.	C.in.d
"	Aug 12	10. am	Inspection of HERMAVILLE & view recent improvements	
		2.30 pm	To attend lecture at AUBIGNY by Col: GREY – Consulting Surgeon III Army.	
		5.0 p.m	To M.D.S. at ECOIVRES & HAUTE AVESNES also H.Q. ASC to have a talk regards co herricomforts	C.in.d

T2134. Wt. W708—776. 500000. 4/15. Sir J. C. & S.

Army Form C. 2118.

WAR DIARY
of
INTELLIGENCE SUMMARY.
(Erase heading not required.)

SHEET IV

Instructions regarding War Diaries and Intelligence Summaries are contained in F. S. Regs, Part II. and the Staff Manual respectively. Title pages will be prepared in manuscript.

Place	Date	Hour	Summary of Events and Information	Remarks and references to Appendices
HERMAVILLE	Aug.13.	11. a.m.	Cook houses and latrines inspected at Convalescent Camp and Entrance School & billets for Reinforcements inspected. HERMAVILLE	
		2.15 p.m.	To NEUVILLE ST VAAST to discuss Medical Arrangements for Defence Scheme with TOWN MAJOR	
			To R.A.Ps on R.t half of L.t Sect.r to discuss enlargements of R.A.Ps. To A.D.S. AUX RIETZ to discuss	
			re-arrangement of Dug-outs.	C.L.T.
"	Aug.14.		Office Routine all day. Two large dug-outs, previously used as billets for 4 R.E.Officers, now handed	
			over to increase accommodation of A.D.S. ANZIN - and reconstruction commenced.	C.L.T.
"	Aug.15.	2.30 p.m.	To AUBIGNY to Conference at D.D.M.S. XVII Corps Office.	
			60.th Divisional R.A.M.C ROUTINE ORDERS nos. 55 to 58 issued.	C.L.T.
"	Aug.16.	10.0 a.m.	To ECURIE to meet Staff Capt. 181.st Infantry Bgde - re. Medical Arrangements for Defence Scheme,	
			Selected Cellars near CHURCH and under house opposite, which will be equipped	
			accordingly.	
			To MAISON BLANCHE to see O.C. Defence Troops of this Brea to discuss medical arrangements	
			re Defence Scheme. Selected Dug-outs which are at present being used as Battalion	
			Head Quarters by Brigade Reserve Battalion.	
		6.30 p.m.	Inspected further constructional work at C.Ps. at ARIANE and MADAGASCAR.	C.L.T.

Army Form C. 2118.

SHEET V

WAR DIARY
INTELLIGENCE SUMMARY.
(Erase heading not required.)

Instructions regarding War Diaries and Intelligence Summaries are contained in F. S. Regs., Part II. and the Staff Manual respectively. Title pages will be prepared in manuscript.

Place	Date	Hour	Summary of Events and Information	Remarks and references to Appendices
HERMAVILLE	Aug.17	1.45 pm	To NEUVILLE ST VAAST to inspect work in progress in new medical trench near GOODMAN TRENCH - To MAISON BLANCHE & inspected accommodation for wounded in tunnels, H.Q. which will be used as R.A.P. in case of an attack. Inspected medical arrangements at A.D.S. AUX RIETZ	(In J)
"	Aug.18	11.0 am.	Inspected Divisional Rear Station at 2/5 London Field Ambulance at HAUTE AVESNES. CAPT. R.H. ASTBURY reported for duty, and temporarily posted for duty with 2/6 London Field Ambulance. CAPT. THORNTON temporarily posted to act as M.O. 1/12 London Regt. Lancers. vice Capt LAING - ill. Issued Medical Arrangements for Scheme of Defence of Reserve Line.	(In J) Appendix 1.
"	Aug.19	11. am	Inspected Convalescent Camp and Gunnar School Camp HERMAVILLE -	
		3.0 pm	Accompanied A.A & Q.M.G. 60th Division and A.D.M.S. XVII Corps to ECOIVRES to discuss medical arrangements and accommodation of 2/4 London Field Ambulance. Capt. HEAD HALL M.O. 2/22 Batt: London Regt: ordered to report forthwith to A.D.M.S. ROUEN - CAPT. FIELD HALL left AUBIGNY at 4.0 p.m. -	(In J)

T2134. Wt. W708—776. 500000. 4/15. Sir J. C. & S.

Army Form C. 2118.

SHEET VI

WAR DIARY
INTELLIGENCE SUMMARY
(Erase heading not required.)

Instructions regarding War Diaries and Intelligence Summaries are contained in F. S. Regs., Part II. and the Staff Manual respectively. Title pages will be prepared in manuscript.

Place	Date	Hour	Summary of Events and Information	Remarks and references to Appendices
HERMAVILLE	Aug 20	11.15 am	With DDMS XVII Corps to inspect Convalescent Camp at HERMAVILLE and 2/5 and 2/6 London Field Ambulance Medical arrangements at HAUTE AVESNES.	
		2.0 pm	To MAROEUIL to inspect an echelon with a view of selecting suitable accommodation for a Divisional Collecting Station in the event of an attack. 60th Division RAMC ROUTINE ORDERS No 59 – 61 issued	C.M.D
	Aug 21	10 am	Visited M.Os Tunnelling Cos R.E. re admission of men to Field Ambulances. Visited 2/4 London Field Ambulance at ECOIVRES re additional accommodation	C.M.D
	Aug 22	2.0 pm	To AUBIGNY for conference at D.D.M.S. Office.	
		5.30 pm	Conference at ADMS Office HERMAVILLE with O.s.C and 2nd in command of 2/4th 2/5th 2/6 London Field Ambulances. Capt J.D.LEGGE CURRIE RAMC and Capt N.PLAINE seconded to Base 2/5 London Field Ambulance. Orders received from D.D.M.S XVII Corps for Lieut MORRIN to report to D.D.M.S VI Corps for duty with gun emmg Coy.	C.M.D
	Aug 23	10.0 am	Inspected ADS ANZIN and C.Ps at MADAGASCAR and ARIANE to view new constructional work. Inspected RAP left half 17 R. SECTOR – 2 RAPs of Centre SECTOR and C.P. at POSTE CENTRALE.	

Army Form C. 2118.

SHEET VII.

WAR DIARY
INTELLIGENCE SUMMARY.
(Erase heading not required.)

Instructions regarding War Diaries and Intelligence Summaries are contained in F. S. Regs., Part II. and the Staff Manual respectively. Title pages will be prepared in manuscript.

Place	Date	Hour	Summary of Events and Information	Remarks and references to Appendices
HERMAVILLE	Aug 23	Cont.	To see Town Major at NEUVILLE ST VAAST to discuss Medical Defence Scheme.	
"	Aug 24	11 am	Inspected new medical trench in R.E. half of L.T Sector. Called on G.O.C. 180/15 Infantry Bgde. Inspected arrangements at A.D.S. AUX RIETZ.	C. in F.
"			Accompanied A.P.A & D.M.S. 60.15 Division to inspect accommodation at MONT ST ELOY - BRAY - MAROEUIL and ETRUN.	C. in D.
"	Aug 25	10.00 am	Accompanied G.O.C. and A.A & Q.M.G. 60.15 Division ECOIVRES to inspect medical arrangements of 2/1 London Field Ambulance	
		2.0 pm	Inspected medical arrangements at M.D.S. AMBALA Field Ambulance at A.C.Q. Inspected A.D.S. ANZIN - Half of 1st Sand bag reinforcement has collapsed - Arrangements made for re-construction.	C. in D.
36	Aug 26	10 am	Inspected medical arrangements at A.D.S. ANZIN - A.D.S. AUX RIETZ and M.I.R. MAROEUIL	C. in D.
"	Aug 27	2.0 pm	To ECURIE to see M.O 2/1 Kent London Regt re medical arrangements of defence Scheme of ECURIE	C. in D.

Army Form C. 2118.

SHEET VIII.

WAR DIARY
INTELLIGENCE SUMMARY.
(Erase heading not required.)

Instructions regarding War Diaries and Intelligence Summaries are contained in F. S. Regs., Part II and the Staff Manual respectively. Title pages will be prepared in manuscript.

Place	Date	Hour	Summary of Events and Information	Remarks and references to Appendices
HERMAVILLE.	Aug 28	10-0am	Visited ECOIVRES with a view to obtaining increased accommodation for 2/4 London Field Ambulance. Lieut FREDERICK MORRES RAMC detailed for duty with 2/5 London Field Ambulance. 60'S Divisional RAMC ROUTINE ORDERS Nos 61 to 66 issued. MEDICAL ARRANGEMENTS IN THE EVENT OF GENERAL ATTACK BY THE ENEMY issued to MOs n ch units - O.C 2/4, 2/5, & 2/6 London Field Ambulances and to O.C Sanitary Section - to Division.	Appendix II
"	Aug 29	2-0pm	To AUBIGNY to attend Conference at DDMS Office	C.h.d -
"	Aug 30	10-am	To HAUTE AVESNES to inspect medical arrangements of 2/5 London Field Ambulance and 2/6 London Field Ambulance.	C.h.d.
		2.30 pm	Course of Lectures on Sanitation and Gas commenced at HERMAVILLE	C.h.d
"	Aug 31	11-0 am	Proceeded to inspect work on new Medical Trench near GOODMAN TRENCH, Inspected A.D.S at AUXRIETZ.	
		4.15 p.m	Conference of M.Os at ADMS Office HERMAVILLE	C.h.d.

E.K.Dowse
COLONEL
ASSISTANT DIRECTOR OF
MEDICAL SERVICES
60TH (LONDON) DIVISION.

APPENDIX I

SECRET

MEDICAL ARRANGEMENTS FOR SCHEME OF DEFENCE OF RESERVE LINE.

Map Reference – Sheets 51^B and 51^C. 1 – 40,000.

No. M/S/23
Date 18·8·16

In the event of an attack by the Germans:-

1. NEUVILLE ST. VAAST.

The Medical Officer in charge of Details in this area will immediately assume complete control of the Collecting Post of the 2/4th Lon. Field Ambce. situated at A.8.b.6.9. and the N.C.O. and 8 men of Field Ambulance permanently stationed there, and of other cellars and dug-outs as below:-

The accommodation is as follows:-

(1.) Large cellar   holding 40 lying cases or 120 Sitting Cases.
(2.) Large French Dug-out. C5.   "   34   "   "   " 90   "   "
(3.) Small Cellar. A9.   "   8   "   "   " 20   "   "
(4.) Small Cellar. A8.   "   8   "   "   " 20   "   "
(5.) Small Cellar. A5.   "   6   "   "   "   8   "   "

The defence being in a series of "Islands", – until such time as these Islands become cut off from one another, all wounded will be brought to (1.) and then to (2) as necessary – after which, as Islands become isolated, all wounded will be collected in a cellar in each, until such time as they can be again concentrated.

All wounded will be evacuated through AUX RIETZ Advanced Dressing Station via DENIS LE ROCK and ROY trenches until no longer possible.

2. MAISON BLANCHE.

The Medical Officer, Pioneer Battalion will immediately go forward from LOUEZ with his Medical Equipment, and all available Battalion Stretcher Bearers and establish his Aid Post at A.14.C.8.5 in the series of Dug-outs at present being used as Battn. H.Q. by the Battalion in Brigade Reserve for Centre Sector.

The accommodation is as follows:-

6 large communicating dug-outs holding 61 lying cases or 130 sitting cases. All wounded would be evacuated through AUX RIETZ Advanced Dressing Station via Trench on E. side BETHUNE Road to Collecting Posts at ARIANE and MADAGASCAR to Adv. Dressing Station at ANZIN until no longer possible.

3. ECURIE.

The Medical Officer of the Battalion in Brigade Reserve of Right Sector will immediately establish his Aid Post in the Vault of the Church situated at H.27.b.6.8. and large Dug-Out opposite (used at present by the Sergt. Major) and take with him his Medical Equipment from the Aid Post at TUNIS.

The accommodation is as follows:-

(1) Church — 24 lying or 50 Sitting.
(2) Dug-Out — 15 lying or 30 Sitting.

All wounded would be evacuated via VILLAGE STREET and MADAGASCAR trenches through MADAGASCAR Collecting Post to ANZIN till no longer possible.

E B Dowell
COLONEL
ASSISTANT DIRECTOR OF
MEDICAL SERVICES
60TH (LONDON) DIVISION.
18.8.16

APPENDIX II

SECRET

MEDICAL ARRANGEMENTS IN THE EVENT OF A GENERAL ATTACK BY THE ENEMY,

additional to the duties ordinarily performed by the Field Ambulances & M.O's of Units.

1. The O's i/c Advanced Dressing Stations at AUX RIETZ and ANZIN on receipt of news and without further orders, will immediately send forward 4 more Bearers to each R.A.P. from which they are collecting, and send to Main Dressing Station or a corresponding number to replace same at Adv. Dressing Station. O's. C. 2/4th & 2/6th London Fd. Ambces. will make all arrangements that these bearers are always available and detailed. This will be carefully arranged at every Relief and the men warned.

2. The O.C. 2/5th London Fd. Ambce., on receipt of orders from A.D.M.S., will send 1 Officer and 40 Other Ranks with 15 Stretchers to Adv. Dressing Station at AUX RIETZ, and 1 Officer and 40 Other Ranks and 15 Stretchers to Adv. Dressing Station at ANZIN to supplement personnel already there. These parties will be permanently detailed and held in readiness. On arrival at Adv. Dressing Stations the senior Officer present will assume Command, and the Bearers will be sent forward to R.A.Ps. as required.

3. The Motor Ambulances of the 2/5th London Fd. Ambce., on an order from A.D.M.S., will be disposed of as follows:-

   4 cars will be sent to the 2/4th London Fd. Ambce. at ECOIVRES, and
   3 cars to the 2/6th London Fd. Ambce. at HAUTE AVESNES, and to be at the disposal of the O's. C. these Units respectively.

4. A <u>DIVISIONAL COLLECTING STATION</u> for walking cases will be formed at MAROEUIL at 18, Ambulance Street, and cellar of No. 13 opposite.

   This Collecting Station will be staffed as follows:-

   M.O. of 60th Divl. R.E. (To Command)
   M.O. of 60th Divl. Ammunition Column.
   M.O. of 60th Divl. Train.
   O.C. Sanitary Section (to supervise evacuation)
   8 Tent-Sub-Divn. men from 2/5th London Fd. Ambce.
       (i.e. 4 dressers - 2 clerks - 2 Cooks)

   1 N.C.O. and 1 man of 2/6th London Fd. Ambce. (permanently in MAROEUIL)

   3 N.C.Os. and 3 men from 60th Divl. Sanitary Section.
       (i.e. for Pack Store - Orderlies - & Evacuation Duties)

   These Officers and parties will be permanently detailed, and will move forward to MAROEUIL on order from A.D.M.S.

4. (Contd) A special and separate A & D Book will be used for the Divisional Collecting Station.

The A & D Book and a large quantity of dressings will be permanently kept at 18, Ambulance Street by the 2/6th London Fd. Ambce. for use in an emergency only.

2 Horsed Ambce. Wagons (with orderlies) from each Field Ambce., and the 60th Divl. Sanitary Section Lorry will be sent to the Divl. Collecting Station on orders from the A.D.M.S. Patients will be evacuated <u>direct</u> to the Casualty Clg. Stations as directed by A.D.M.S., the very slightly wounded being despatched on foot under an Officer or N.C.O.

5. Medical Officers of all Battalions & Artillery Groups, will especially note that all Walking Cases must be sent <u>direct</u> to the Divl. Collecting Station at MAROEUIL and not through the Advanced Dressing Stations.

MEDICAL ARRANGEMENTS IN THE EVENT OF A GENERAL ATTACK BY THE 60th DIVISION.

(Additional to the duties ordinarily performed) are <u>as above</u> with the following addition:—

M.O's. of all Battalions in the front line will move forward to the Advanced Regtl. Aid Posts which have been previously selected. Each of these Advanced Posts will be clearly marked with a Red Cross several days before the Attack, or as long before as Attack Orders will allow. All concerned must be conversant with the Situation selected.

G. B. Dowse
COLONEL.
A.D.M.S. 60th (LONDON) DIVISION.

H.Q. 60th DIVISION.
AUGUST 25th 1916.

Sept 19/16

ADM 86 D
Vol 4

Confidential.

War Diary (Medical).
of
60th (London) Division.

From Sept 1-16 to Sept 30-16.
Volume

COMMITTEE FOR THE
MEDICAL HISTORY OF THE WAR
Date 26 OCT 1915

E Bousted
A.D.M.S. 60th (London) Division.
Colonel.

ORIGINAL.

MEDICAL.

Army Form C. 2118.

WAR DIARY
or
INTELLIGENCE SUMMARY.
(Erase heading not required.)

Instructions regarding War Diaries and Intelligence Summaries are contained in F. S. Regs., Part II. and the Staff Manual respectively. Title pages will be prepared in manuscript.

Place	Date	Hour	Summary of Events and Information	Remarks and references to Appendices
HERMAVILLE	Sept 1	11 am	To inspect M.D.S. 2/15 London Field Ambulance at HAUTEAVESNES.	
		2.15 pm	To inspect Cooking & Sanitary arrangements of the 60th Division R.A.C. at FREVIN CAPELLE. ETRUN & helped.	C.in.J
	Sept 2	10 a.m.	To inspect A.D.S. ANZIN – and the arrangements of M.I.R. & 18 AMBULANCE ST MAROEUIL	C.in.J
	Sept 3	10 a.m.	To inspect MDS 2/4 London Field Ambulance at ECOIVRES – with a view to obtaining more accommodation.	
			To inspect MDS of 2/5 and 2/6 London Field Ambulances at HAUTE AVESNES.	C.in.J.
	Sept 4		War diaries forwarded.	
		1.30 pm	To M.D.S. 2/4 London Field Ambulance with reference to Daily State A.F.W. 3155.	
		2.15 pm	To 18 AMBULANCE ST MAROEUIL – Medical Board on P.B. and other men – President.	
			A.D.M.S. 60th Division MEMBERS, MAJOR FEGEN R.A.M.C., CAPT THORNTON R.A.M.C.	C.in.J.
	Sept 5	10.30 a.m.	To inspect medical arrangements at 2/4 London Field Ambulance M.D.S. at ECOIVRES.	
		10.30 a.m.	D A D M S 60th Div. accompanied DADMS (SAN) III Army and DADMS XVII CORPS (with O.C. Sanitary Section) to inspect condition of dug-outs at ANZIN and near MADAGASCAR.	
		2.30 pm	Conference of DDMS XVII CORPS Office at AUBIGNY.	
			Capt C.M. LLOYD R.A.M.C. – T.C. reported for duty – ordered for temporary duty with 2/4 Lon: Field Ambulance.	C.in.J

Army Form C. 2118.

WAR DIARY
INTELLIGENCE SUMMARY.
(Erase heading not required.)

Place	Date	Hour	Summary of Events and Information	Remarks and references to Appendices
HERMAVILLE	Sept 6	8.45am to 2-0pm	With C.R.E. to inspect new Medical Trench near GOODMAN TRENCH and to obtain advice on best method of drainage of and for laying out in same. Inspected R.A.P. at LA PARTIRVE.	Ch. I
"	Sept 7	10 am	To LATRISSET to inspect proposed new hover-lines for R.F.A. ORDERS received from D.D.M.S. XVII Corps for CAPT. S.M. LLOYD R.A.M.C. to report at once for duty with 54th Field Ambulance at BAILLEUL and CORNAILLES (CAPT LLOYD left area for duty with 5/65 Field Ambulance). LIEUT. F. MORRES 2/5 London Field Ambulance to report at once for duty with 5/65 Field Ambulance at L'ABBAYE LE NEUVILLE OSTREVILLE. LIEUT F MORRES left.	Ch. II
			bo/o Division R.A.M.C. ROUTINE ORDERS no 67 to 70 issued.	
"	Sept 8	10.30am to 3.30pm	D.A.D.M.S. bath Division with DADMS XVII CORPS proceeded to ST MICHEL SUR TERNOISE to inspect XVII CORPS LAUNDRY, and methods of dealing with foul and verminous clothing.	
		2-0 pm	To inspect A.D.S. AVIZIN - To inspect MRS at ECOIVRES.	
	Sept 9	9.15am to 2.30pm	To RAP of Left Bder of Centre Sect. To inspect new internal construction work - Baths inspected at NEUVILLE ST VAAST	
		3.30pm	Accompanied D.D.M.S. XVII CORPS and Lt. Col. Sir L ORMSBEY - Consulting Physician WELSH Division M.D.Ss on ECOIVRES and HAUTE AVESNES and to ADS at AVIZIN.	Ch. 3

WAR DIARY or INTELLIGENCE SUMMARY

Army Form C. 2118.

Place	Date	Hour	Summary of Events and Information	Remarks and references to Appendices
HERMAVILLE	Sept 10	8.20am	DADMS 60th Division proceeded to ST POL to attend short course on ANTI GAS MEASURES.	
"		3.0pm	To HAUTE AVESNES to inspect medical arrangements at D.R.S 2/5 London Field Ambulance.	Cont.
"	Sept 11	10.0am	Accompanied ADMS 60th Division to ECOIVRES to see the Field Ambulance and to inspect accommodation of 9 PMS of 2/4 London Field Ambulance there. To inspect A.S.C. Quarters at HAUTE AVESNES.	
"		2.0pm	MEDICAL BOARD on P.B. men and others at 180th Bde Rear Head Quarters at MONT ST ELOY. President ADMS 60th Division - Members Major FEGEN RAMC & Capt THORNTON RAMC.	Cont.
"	Sept 12	10.30am	Conference at D.D.M.S. XVII CORPS OFFICE AUBIGNY 60th Division RAMC ROUTINE ORDERS No 71, 672, 673 issued	Cont.
"	Sept 13	8.45am	Visited RAP Left Redd. Left Sector and RAP Right Redd. Left Sector. Inspected work in progress in new Medical Dugout and Trolley line near GOBSMAN TRENCH. Inspected CENOT CAVE and RAP LA PORTIQUE	
		to	Reconnoitred several trenches with a view to the evacuation of wounded from extreme Right of Left Sector.	
		4.30pm	Inspected A.D.S. AVRIETZ - Called on R.H. of 9/180th Brigade on the question of the transport of Vermorel Sprayers.	
		12.30pm	DADMS 60th Division accompanied DADMS XVII Corps and O.C. 60th Division Sanitary Section proceeded to D.M.S. 1st Army - to inspect Sanitary and other appliances and the local incinerators and destructors in use at LILLERS.	Cont.

Army Form C. 2118.

WAR DIARY
INTELLIGENCE SUMMARY.
(Erase heading not required.)

Instructions regarding War Diaries and Intelligence Summaries are contained in F. S. Regs., Part II. and the Staff Manual respectively. Title pages will be prepared in manuscript.

Place	Date	Hour	Summary of Events and Information	Remarks and references to Appendices
HERMAVILLE	Sept 14	11.0 am	Accompanied by DDMS XVII Corps made reconnaissance of whole of Left Sector with regard to the evacuation of	
		6.0 pm	Trenches for the evacuation of wounded from front line to Existing R.A.Ps. Report forwarded 15 H. & 61st Sanitarian	C.h.J
		2.0 pm	Course on Sanitation and gas measures at Convalescent Camp HERMAVILLE	
"	Sept 15	11.0 am	Conference at DDMS XVII Corps B.E.G.C. AUBIGNY	
		2.0 pm	Course on Sanitation and gas measures continued	
		2.0 pm	To inspect R.A.P. AVIZY and new construction work Khaki	
		3.45 pm	Conference of MOs 60th Division at ADMS Office HERMAVILLE	C.h.Q
"	Sept 16	9.0 am	Reconnoitred Right half of Left Sector with a view to finding site for new R.A.P. and fresh Evacuation Trenches	
	to		in case of an action. Found Small cave due E. of CENOTAVE at A.3.b.2.3 which it was preferable for	
		4.0 pm	Supplementary A.P. Evacuation to Same by FOURCHE TRENCH	
		6.0 pm	To AUBIGNY to report this to D.A.M.S. XVII Corps.	C.h.J
"	Sept 17	2.0 pm	Inspected Kitchens and Sanitary arrangements of 1/5 Left Artillery Group.	C.h.J
"	Sept 18		Orders issued for CAPT DRAKE BROCKMAN RAMC — CAPT HOWLETT RAMC and Lieut SINCLAIR to	
			Report at once to ADMS GUARDS DIVISION 4th Army. These Officers proceeded at 9.0 am.	
		10.30 am	To Inspect MDS at ECOIVRES.	C.h.J
			60th Division RAMC ROUTINE ORDERS No 74 Issued	

Army Form C. 2118.

WAR DIARY
INTELLIGENCE SUMMARY
(Erase heading not required.)

Instructions regarding War Diaries and Intelligence Summaries are contained in F.S. Regs., Part II. and the Staff Manual respectively. Title pages will be prepared in manuscript.

Place	Date	Hour	Summary of Events and Information	Remarks and references to Appendices
HERMAVILLE	Sept 19	2.30 pm	Conference at D.D.M.S Office AUBIGNY.	C.in.J
"			Capt COLE M.O. Detail Evacuation Sick from C.C.S.	
"	Sept 20	10 am	To A.D.S. AUXRIETZ & to inspect progress of work at new medical Trench - Also to inspect new Structural Work at M.D.S. 2/4 London Field Ambulance at ECOIVRES	C.in.J.
"		4. pm		
"	Sept 21	10.0 am	Accompanied A.D.M.S 60th Division to inspect 2/5 & 2/6 London Field Ambulances at HAUTEAVESNES - 2/4 London Field Ambulance at ECOIVRES - 1st CONVALESCENT CAMP and 60th Divi Sanitary Section at HERMAVILLE.	
"		2.15 pm	To A.D.S. AUXRIETZ and to inspect new medical Trench near GOODMAN TRENCH - to inspect R.A.P. L.I. and 15 Battl: H.Q. at LA PORTIQUE to see M.OS Discussed New Exit for C.P. at NEUVILLE ST VAAST of 2/4 London Field Ambulance.	C.in.J
"	Sept 22	10.15 am	To MONT ST ELOY to meet D.M.S. 1st Army and D.D.M.S XVII Corps to inspect M.D.S of 2/4 London Field Ambulance at ECOIVRES - 2/5 London Field Ambulance D.R.S. at HAUTE AVESNES and M.D.S. of 2/6 London Field Ambulance at HAUTE AVESNES. CONVALESCENT CAMP and 60th Division Sanitary Section Workshop and Exhibits at HERMAVILLE - 60th Division R.A.M.C. ROUTINE ORDERS N° 75&79 issued -	C.in.J.

Army Form C. 2118.

WAR DIARY
INTELLIGENCE SUMMARY.
(Erase heading not required.)

Instructions regarding War Diaries and Intelligence Summaries are contained in F. S. Regs., Part II. and the Staff Manual respectively. Title pages will be prepared in manuscript.

Place	Date	Hour	Summary of Events and Information	Remarks and references to Appendices
HERMAVILLE	Sept 23	12.15 pm	By order of D.M.S. 1st Army, accompanied by D.C. 60th Div: Sanitary Section proceeded to LA GORGUE to visit Sanitary Section workshop of 61st Division and to inspect methods of working and appliances constructed in it	C in D
"	Sept 24	2-0 pm	Inspected A.R.S. of 1/1 London Field Ambulance at HAUTE PUESNES. Proceeded to Rear H.Q. 160th Inf. Brigade to discuss Returns of Sick	
			Inspected S.U.E. for Div: Collecting Station at MAROEUIL	C in D
"	Sept 25	2-0 pm	Conference at D.D.M.S. XVII Corps Office at AUBIGNY	C in D
"	Sept 26	9.30 am	Inspected C.P. at ROUTE DELILLE and R.A.P. at R.1. to view new internal constructional work for shelter next S.O. - work progressing well.	
		4-2.30 pm	Visited R.A.P. at R.2.	
			Inspected Refuse dump at MINOTAUR TRENCH and the newfalls dug there.	C in D.
"	Sept 27	8.0 am	Inspected new constructional work at A.D.S. at AUXRIETZ - Discussed with C.R.E. on the spot, the feasibility of a water supply being laid on to it	
		6.15 pm	Div: Routine ORDERS no 80 to 81 issued.	C in D

Army Form C. 2118.

WAR DIARY
INTELLIGENCE SUMMARY.
(Erase heading not required.)

Instructions regarding War Diaries and Intelligence Summaries are contained in F.S. Regs., Part II. and the Staff Manual respectively. Title pages will be prepared in manuscript.

VII

Place	Date	Hour	Summary of Events and Information	Remarks and references to Appendices
HERMAVILLE	Sept 28	10.0 am	To HAUTE AVESNES to inspect D.R.S. 2/5 London Field Ambulance and to ECOIVRES to inspect M.D.S. 2/4 London Field Ambulance and the constructional work now being carried on there	C.L. D
"	Sept 29	2-6 pm	To Divisional Baths at MAROEUIL. Arranged that 20 of 152 men now employed there be replaced by 20 R.A.M.C. men, the replaced men being returned to their respective Units. To see O.C. 181st Brigade to discuss use of Light Railway in his sector for the evacuation of wounded. Received memo. D.M.S. P.L.9.6.4 - from D.M.S. 1st Army re reduction, as a temporary measure, of establishment of Field Ambulance M.O.s. to 7.	C.L. D
"	Sept 30	10. am	Inspected new kitchen in course of construction at A.D.S. AUX RIETZ and C.P. see NEUVILLE ST VAAST and POSTE CENTRALE Discussed further use of Light Railway with O.C. 2/6 London Field Ambulance in the area.	C.L. D

[Signature]
COLONEL
ASSISTANT DIRECTOR OF
MEDICAL SERVICES
60TH (LONDON) DIVISION.

Oct. 1916

Confidential

Vol 5
140/11/50

War Diary (Medical)
A.D.M.S. 60th (London) Division.
From 1st October 1916 to 31 October 1916.

Volume.

COMMITTEE FOR THE
MEDICAL HISTORY OF THE WAR
Date —2 DEC. 1916

E R Dorsett
Colonel.
A.D.M.S. 60 (London) Division

MEDICAL.
Army Form C. 2118.

SHEET I.

WAR DIARY
INTELLIGENCE SUMMARY.
(Erase heading not required.)

Instructions regarding War Diaries and Intelligence Summaries are contained in F. S. Regs., Part II. and the Staff Manual respectively. Title pages will be prepared in manuscript.

Place	Date	Hour	Summary of Events and Information	Remarks and references to Appendices
HERMAVILLE	OCT 1	9.15AM	Inspected R.A.P.s ANZIN. Inspected site in forward area of Centre Sector for possible new R.A.P.s. No existing dug-outs available or suitable to convert.	
			Visited G.O.C. 179th Infantry Bgde to discuss question of using 40 c.m. railways in Centre Sector for evacuation of wounded.	(h.d)
"	OCT 2	4.30pm		
		2-0pm	Conference at A.D.M.S.(XVII Corps) AUBIGNY.	
			Lieut D.A. THOMPSON, T.C. reported for duty from England — Posted to 2/5 London Field Ambulance	
			Capt A.J.C. TINGEY, T.C. reported for duty from 50th Regt R.G.A. Posted to 1/12 Loyal North Lancs.	
			Lieut E.W. ATKINSON, T.C. reported for duty from No 26 General Hospital. Posted to 2/5 London Field Ambulance.	(h.d)
"	OCT 3	2-0pm	Medical Board on PB and other men at No 18 Ambulance at MAROEUIL. President A.D.M.S — Prestwton	
			Major FEGEN R.A.M.C. and Capt THORNTON R.A.M.C.	
"			Capt C.M. KELLORTE reported for duty from No 23 General Hospital. Posted for duty to 2/6 London Field Ambulance	
			Lieut A.J.P. NOWELL T.C. reported from No 11 General Hospital — Posted for duty to 1/5 London Field Ambulance	(h.d)
"	OCT 4	8.30 AM	A.D.M.S. proceeded on leave	
		2.0pm	Medical Board at CONVALESCENT CAMP. HERMAVILLE — President Lt.Col. BIRD D.S.O. Members — Major FEGEN R.A.M.C. Capt THORNTON R.A.M.C.	(h.d)

Army Form C. 2118.

WAR DIARY
INTELLIGENCE SUMMARY.
(Erase heading not required.)

SHEET II

Instructions regarding War Diaries and Intelligence Summaries are contained in F. S. Regs., Part II. and the Staff Manual respectively. Title pages will be prepared in manuscript.

Place	Date	Hour	Summary of Events and Information	Remarks and references to Appendices
HERMAVILLE	Oct 5	11.30am	DADMS 6th Inson Division to see ADMS XVII Corps at AUBIGNY	C.h.J
"			WAR DIARIES sent in	C.h.J
"	Oct 6	3.0pm	DADMS XVII Corps inspected Sanitary Exhibits at CONVALESCENT CAMP, HERMAVILLE	
"	Oct 7	11.0am	DADMS accompanied A.D.C. 60th London Division to inspect medical arrangements of 2/4 London	C.h.J
"			Field Ambulance at M.D.S. at ECOIVRES	
"	Oct 8	2.30pm	DADMS to R.D.M.S XVII Corps AUBIGNY	C.h.J
"	Oct 9		Office routine	C.h.J
"	Oct 10		Office routine	C.h.J
"	Oct 11	10.0am	DADMS to see O.C. 2/5 London Field Ambulance re cases of Scabies	
			O.C. 2/6 London Field Ambulance proceeded on leave	
			Capt THORNTON 4/6 London Field Ambulance is posted for temporary duty as M.O. 2/4 Essex (London Regt).	
			Capt BELL M.O. 2/4 Essex Regt joins for temporary duty with 4/6 London Field Ambulance	
			Orders received from DMS 1st ARMY for two Medical Officers to report for duty IC to A-D.M.S. VIII Division for duty.	
			Lieut EW ATKINSON T.C. and Lieut A P NOWELL T.C. left to report to A.D.M.S. VIII Division for duty	
		5.30pm	ADMS returned from leave	
			Issued instructions A.D.M.S. 60th Division acts as D.Q.M.S. XII Corps during absence on leave of D.D.M.S. until	C.h.J
			OTW 2.0.16	

Army Form C. 2118.

SHEET III

WAR DIARY
INTELLIGENCE SUMMARY.
(Erase heading not required.)

Instructions regarding War Diaries and Intelligence Summaries are contained in F. S. Regs., Part II. and the Staff Manual respectively. Title pages will be prepared in manuscript.

Place	Date	Hour	Summary of Events and Information	Remarks and references to Appendices
HERMAVILLE	Oct 12	11.5am	Received verbal instruction from XVII CORPS as to new Scheme of Attack of probably 3 Division	
			Attended DDMS OFFICE at AUBIGNY as acting DDMS XVII Corps	
		2.0pm	Course on Sanitation and Antigas measures commenced.	C. h. J.
"	Oct 13	10.30am	Visit DADMS XVII Corps to reconnoitre means of evacuation and sites for ADSs for the whole of the Corps front likely to be in action on the new Scheme. Selected site for new A.D.S. on BETHUNE ROAD where PONT ST CROSSES Same for Left Division – Also reconnoitred new C.P.S. and new means of evacuation for Right Division of new Scheme	
			Received instructions from H.Q. 60th Division re Scheme of attack for one Brigade of 60th London Division	C. h. J.
		2.0pm	Course on Sanitation and Antigas measures continued.	
"	Oct 14		To D.D.M.S. Office AUBIGNY.	
			As acting D.D.M.S. XVII Corps forwarded Scheme of medical arrangements for the whole of the Corps Scheme of attack before mentioned.	C. h. J.
			Forwarded to H.Q. 60th Division Scheme of medical arrangements for before mentioned Scheme of attack	Appendix 1
"	Oct 15		DADMS (Sany) 1st Army and DADMS XVII Corps – with DADMS 60th Division inspected 60th Division Sanitary Section Workshops and exhibition also sanitary arrangements at 2/5 & 2/6 London Field Ambulance M.D.S. at HAUTE AVESNES – CONVALESCENT CAMP at HERMAVILLE and at ST ELOY	C. h. J.

WAR DIARY
INTELLIGENCE SUMMARY

Army Form C. 2118.

SHEET IV

Instructions regarding War Diaries and Intelligence Summaries are contained in F. S. Regs., Part II. and the Staff Manual respectively. Title pages will be prepared in manuscript.

(Erase heading not required.)

Place	Date	Hour	Summary of Events and Information	Remarks and references to Appendices
HERMAVILLE	Oct 16	10.0 am	To A.D.S. AUX RIETZ and C.P. at NEUVILLE ST VAAST to inspect new constructional work	C.L.T.
"	Oct 17	10.0 am	To D.R.S. L/s London Field Ambulance at HAUTE AVESNES to inspect M.D.S. and new cooking arrangements and sanitary arrangements	C.L.T.
"	Oct 18	9.0 am	D.A.D.M.S. 61st Division left for seven days leave to ENGLAND.	
		11.30 am	To D.D.M.S. XVII Corps office at AUBIGNY.	
		2.30 pm	To ECOIVRES to inspect M.D.S. and new outhouses of 2/4 London Field Ambulance.	E.N.D.
"	Oct 19	2-6 pm	MEDICAL BOARD on all N.C.O's and men remaining in Convalescent Camp HERMAVILLE. Authorised those "unfit" for Service at the Front" to be sent to their Base Depôts. Remainder to be sent with to Field Ambulances for treatment or to be returned to their units	(A.)
			Received Divisional Order No 2 re: Short to new area.	
"	Oct 20		A.D.M.S. 3rd CANADIAN DIVISION visited this area. Conducted him to all Field Ambulance & M.D.S's and to A.D.S. AVZIN.	
			Explained fully the system of evacuation on whole of Divisional Front.	
			Issued 60th Division R.A.M.C. operation orders to all Field Ambulance & M.D.S.	Appendix 2.

Army Form C. 2118.

SHEET V

WAR DIARY
INTELLIGENCE SUMMARY
(Erase heading not required.)

Instructions regarding War Diaries and Intelligence Summaries are contained in F.S. Regs., Part II. and the Staff Manual respectively. Title pages will be prepared in manuscript.

Place	Date	Hour	Summary of Events and Information	Remarks and references to Appendices
HERMAVILLE	Oct 21.	11. am	1 Officer, 1 N.C.O. and 4 men from 8th, 9th, 10th Canadian Field Ambulances reported at this Office and were sent to 2/6, 2/4 & 2/5 London Field Ambulances respectively to remain and learn working and sanitation areas. Interviewed A.D. (Brigade Major) re medical arrangements on line of route. (E.P.D.)	
"	Oct 22		Issued to 10th Divisional R.A.M.C. Operation Order No 4 & re Surplus Stores in each Field Ambulance.	Appendix 3
			Issued all necessary orders re Ambulance Wagon following in rear of each Brigade on march to new area and for the transforms of any sick. (E.P.D.)	Appendix 4
"	Oct 23		Visited A.D.S. at AUXMETZ and R.A.P. at Left Sector 2.	
			Two sections of each 8th, 9th & 10th London Field Ambulances reported.	
			2/6, 2/4 & 2/5 London Field Ambulances respectively -	
			Hd A.D.S. and Collecting Posts and R.A.P. relieved by Canadians by 6.0 p.m. -	
			Main Dressing Stations and Divisional Rear Station taken over by 9.0 p.m. - (E.P.D.)	
"	Oct 24		All London Field Ambulances moved off to new area.	
			2/4 London Field Ambulance arrived at MONT-EN-TERNOIS at 3 p.m.	
			2/5 " " " arrived at PENIN at 1 p.m.	
			2/6 " " " arrived at SUS ST LEGER at 4 p.m.	
			Lieut W.A. HOTSON T.C. and Lieut L. LESLIE T.C. reported for duty. Ordered for temporary duty to 2/6 North Midland Field Ambulance. (E.P.D.)	

Army Form C. 2118.

SHEET VI

WAR DIARY
INTELLIGENCE SUMMARY.
(Erase heading not required.)

Instructions regarding War Diaries and Intelligence Summaries are contained in F.S. Regs., Part II and the Staff Manual respectively. Title pages will be prepared in manuscript.

Place	Date	Hour	Summary of Events and Information	Remarks and references to Appendices
HERMAVILLE	Oct 24	Cont	All medical arrangements handed over to ADMS 32nd Canadian Division at noon -	e.n.d.
"	Oct 25	11-a.m	Received 60th Division Orders No 3 and 4 Visited all Field Ambulances in new area - Arrangements made for its reception of sick of Brigade in each area Received receipts from Field Ambulances of all Stores etc handed over to incoming Canadian Field Ambulances.	e.n.d.
		5·0 p.m	D.A.D.M.S. 60th London Division arrived back from leave.	
Houvin Houvigneul	Oct 26	10·0 a.m	60th Division Head Quarters moved to HOUVIN HOUVIGNEUL	
		11·0	Opened Office	
		2.30 p.m	To 2/4 London Field Ambulance to inspect medical arrangements at MONTS-EN-TERNOISE	C.M.♂
"	Oct 27	11·0 a.m	Visited and inspected medical arrangements of and made arrangements for evacuation of sick by 2/4th London Field Ambulance at MONTS-EN-TERNOIS 2/5 " " " " MONCHEUX 2/6 " " " " SUS-ST-LEGER	C.M.♂ C.M.♂
FROHEN LE GRAND	Oct 28	9·0 a.m	Head Quarters 60th London Division moved to FROHEN LE GRAND All motor Ambulances and motor cyclists left Field Ambulances.	C.M.♂

Army Form C. 2118.

S. HEFT VII

WAR DIARY
or
INTELLIGENCE SUMMARY.
(Erase heading not required.)

Instructions regarding War Diaries and Intelligence Summaries are contained in F. S. Regs., Part II. and the Staff Manual respectively. Title pages will be prepared in manuscript.

Place	Date	Hour	Summary of Events and Information	Remarks and references to Appendices
FROBERVIEGRAND HQRS Fort			2/6 London Field Ambulance moved to NEVILLE - Reception Hospital opened	
	2/4		" " " " " " FORTEL " " "	
	2/5		" " " " " " REBRAISNIL " " "	
BERNAVILLE	Oct 29	9.0 am	60 (1st) London Division H.Q. moved to BERNAVILLE.	
		10 am	Office opened	
"	Oct 30	12 noon	Visited and inspected medical arrangements of and arranged for evacuation of sick by	
			2/6 London Field Ambulance at MON PLAISIR.	
		3	" " " " " " PROUVILLE.	
		4 pm	" " " " " " " "	
		2/5	" " " " " " LE MEILLARD	
"	Oct 31	11-30 am	Spoke to Capt B. BARRETT, D.A.D.M.S. 60th Division; suffering from a severe attack of neuralgia to	
			No. 19 C.C.S. DOULENS for evacuation	

S.B.Dowse
COLONEL
ASSISTANT DIRECTOR OF
MEDICAL SERVICES
60TH (LONDON) DIVISION.

Copy. Appendix I   Secret.

SCHEME OF MEDICAL ARRANGEMENTS DURING OPERATIONS ON FRONT FROM
A. 4. d. 2. 2. to A. 4. a. 5. 2. (Approximately).

1. REGIMENTAL AID POSTS.

   Must be found by Battalion in neighbourhood of Support Line and as
   near down trenches as possible, somewhere on the line from A.10.a-5.9.
   to A.4.c.1.8. So far, no convenient dug-outs have been selected.

2. FIELD AMBULANCE COLLECTING POSTS.

   (i) 2 Cellars - E.18 and E. 19 - at A.9.b.2.9. This to have 1
   Field Ambulance Medical Officer and Relays of bearers to carry from
   R.A.P's.

   Wheeled stretcher carriages would be kept here to use on THELUS Road
   to AUX RIETZ by night, and also by day if no barrage of fire preventing

   (N.B.- The reason for having Medical Officer here is that the
   accommodation for the forward R.A.P's would be so limited that many
   cases would have to be sent on without M.O's attention, which they
   could then receive here.)

   (ii) Shelter at A.9.a.2.1. where RIETZ Trench crosses N. End of
   ELBE Trench. This to have further relays of bearers and large number
   of wheeled stretcher carriages.

3. ADVANCED DRESSING STATION.

   AUX RIETZ at A.8.c.2.2.

4. WALKING WOUNDED COLLECTING POST.

   MAROEUIL at 18, ECURIE Street, at F.28.c.1.3.

   (N.B.- Also small relays of bearers here to answer calls from
   Heavy Artillery Groups.)

5. MAIN DRESSING STATIONS.

   (i) ECOIVRES at F.13.b.3.5. (2/4th London Field Ambulance.)

   (ii) HAUTE AVESNES at E.28.c.9.9. (2/6th London Field Ambulance).

   (N.B.- Wounded would be evacuated to (i) first, until full, and
   then diverted to (ii).).

6. EVACUATION.

   (a) From forward R.A.P's. - by Field Ambulance Bearers via DENIS LE ROCK
       trench or RIETZ Trench to Collecting Post (i) as above.

   (b) From Collecting Post (i) - by further relays of bearers either
       by the THELUS Road direct to AUX RIETZ by wheeled stretcher
       carriage, or by hand carriage via RIETZ Trench.

   (c) From Collecting Post (ii) - either by wheeled stretcher carriage
       by pathway and road, or by hand carriage via RIETZ Trench to
       AUX RIETZ.

- 2 -

(d) <u>From A.D.S. at AUX RIETZ.</u> - Stretcher cases may have to be held up here till night fall. If, however, circumstances permit, such cases would be sent down by day on wheeled stretcher carriages or by Motor Ambulance Cars via MAROEUIL to ECOIVRES. In any case the wheeled stretcher cases can be picked up by Cars at BRUNEHAUT FARM.

If circumstances permit, cases would be evacuated from AUX RIETZ by the light Medical trollies or the down stores trollies on the 60 cm. railway to BOIS DE BRAY and there picked up by Motor Ambulance Cars. These trollies would be man-handled and arrangements made direct with O.i/c. Light Railways so as not to interfere with the Up Traffic.

(e) <u>Walking Wounded</u> - All walking wounded would be ~~evacuated~~ encouraged by M.O's of Units and at Collecting Posts to walk to MAROEUIL so as not to congest the A.D.S. From MAROEUIL all cases would be sent direct to the C.C.S. at AUBIGNY so as not to congest the Main Dressing Stations.

(f) <u>Transport</u> - All Field Ambulance Cars and Wagons will work between A.D.S. and Main Dressing Station, and in advance of Walking Wounded Post.

Corps Ambulance Convoy Cars will work between Main Dressing Stations and C.C.S. and also between Walking Wounded Post and C.C.S.

APPENDIX.

WORK TO BE DONE PRIOR TO SCHEME BEING FULLY WORKABLE :-

<u>Approx. Estimate of Work.</u>

1. Clearing of down trenches to take Stretchers, and duck-boarding in parts.   50 men - 7 days.

2. Collecting Post (i) - Knocking down of part of wall to allow entrance of stretchers to cellars, and also internal adaption.   6 men - 7 days.

3. Preparation of Walking Wounded Post.   Fd.Amb. Tent-Sub-Division. 1 day.

4. Road to be cleared of rubbish and holes filled in between A.9.a.3.9. and A.9.a.6.7.; also 2 trenches to be bridged in this part.   10 men - 1 night.
The bridges are already prepared.

2, 3 & 4 can easily be done by Field Ambulance Bearers at any time, but 1, would require expert assistance.

H.Q. 60th Division.   (Sd) E. B. DOWSETT. Colonel.
October 14th 1916.   A.D.M.S. 60th (London) Division.

SECRET.   **APPENDIX II**   COPY. No. 4

R.A.M.C. OPERATION ORDER No 3.

October 20th 1916.

1. The 60th Division (less Artillery) will be relieved by the 3rd Canadian Division (less Artillery) during the period 23 - 26 October, 1916.

   The 60th Division is to be concentrated in the new area by midnight 27 - 28 October 1916.

2. Os./C. Field Ambulances will hand over the Command of the Medical Arrangements of their respective areas on completion of relief. Completion of relief of each Unit to be reported to this Office.

3. March Table and Schedule of reliefs will be issued later.

4. Refilling Points will be detailed later.

5. The Command of the Front remains in the hands of the G.O.C. 60th Division until 10 am 26th inst., at which hour 60th Divl. H.Q. will open at LE CAUROY.

6. Receipts will be received for any stores, including Red Cross Stores, from Os./C. incoming Field Ambulances in accordance with H.Q. memorandum C/371 of the 19th inst., copy being forwarded to this Office.

7. Patients left in 60th Divisional Field Ambulances will be shown in the A.&D. Books as "Transferred to Canadian Field Ambulances", and Nominal Roll with all necessary particulars will be handed to the Os./C. respective relieving Field Ambulances.

8. Details to be arranged by Os./C concerned.

9. Acknowledge.

E.R.Dowsett
COLONEL.
A.D.M.S. 60th (LONDON) DIVISION.

Copy No 1. O.C. 2/4th Lon. Fd. Amb.
"   2.   O.C. 2/5th Lon. Fd. Amb.
"   3.   O.C. 2/6th Lon. Fd. Amb.
"   4.   War Diary.
"   5.   Duplicate War Diary.
"   6.   File.

APPENDIX III

Copy No. 4

SECRET.

60th DIVISION R.A.M.C. OPERATION ORDER No. 4

Ref. Map LENS - Sheet 11.

October 22nd 1916

1. The reliefs of Field Ambulances and their marches to new Area will be carried out in accordance with Tables "A" & "D" attached.
   All arrangements as to guides to front area will be made by Os.C. Field Ambulances concerned.

2. All incoming parties of Canadian Field Ambulance on 23rd inst. will be rationed and billeted by the respective London Field Ambulance to which they are attached, till relief is complete.
   Arrangements will be made for the billeting by closing up the patients into fewer huts for night of 23rd - 24th October, 1916, and utilising a hut for the personnel.

3. The actual destination and billeting accommodation of each Field Ambulance in its new area must be forthwith ascertained by Os.C. from the respective Brigades to which they are attached (vide Table "D").

4. A temporary receiving station for sick will be opened by each Field Ambulance immediately on arrival in the new area, and the Brigade Offices in the respective areas informed.
   All sick not likely to be well in 24 hours will be transferred direct to No. 12 Stationary Hospital, ST. POL.

5. Separate instructions are being issued re Field Ambulance Stores. See Operation Order No. 3 re receipts.

6. On evening of 22nd inst. each Field Ambulance will send four Ambulance Wagons, with orderlies, (3 horsed & 1 motor) - one to each of the Wagons lines of the Battalions of the respective Brigades to which the Field Ambulances are attached. These will remain with the Battalions till arrival in New Area, when they will return to their Units.
   The wagons will be under the orders of the M.O's of Units, and are for the purpose of collecting sick on line of route. Before leaving, Os.C. Field Ambulances will instruct the wagon orderlies that they are only to pick up men possessing a chit signed by the M.O. of the Unit.

7. Command of the Medical Arrangements of present 60th Division Area will be handed over to A.D.M.S. 3rd Canadian Division at Noon 24th inst.

8. Acknowledge.

EBDowse
Colonel.
A.D.M.S. 60th (London) Division.

Copy No. 1   2/4th Lon. Fd. Amb.
Copy No. 2   2/5th Lon. Fd. Amb.
Copy No. 3   2/6th Lon. Fd. Amb.
Copy No. 4   War Diary.
Copy No. 5   Duplicate War Diary.
Copy No. 6   File.
Copy No. 7   Headquarters.

TABLE A

RELIEF TABLE OF FIELD AMBULANCES OF 60th (LONDON) DIVISION.

Unit	Proceeding to	Time of arrival	Relieves	Proceeding to	Time of Departure
8th CANADIAN FIELD AMBULANCE. 1 Officer) 4 N.C.O's) 40 men)	ANZIN and Right Sector trenches via HAUTE AVESNES.	About noon at HAUTE AVESNES Oct.23rd 1918	2/6th Lon Fd Amb personnel at Adv. Dressing Station and in front of same.	HAUTE AVESNES	When relieved
9th CANADIAN FIELD AMBULANCE. 1 Officer) 4 N.C.O's) 40 men)	AUX RIETZ and left and centre sectors trenches via ECOIVRES.	About noon at ECOIVRES Oct.23rd 1918	2/4th Lon Fd Amb personnel at Adv. Dressing Station and infront of same.	ECOIVRES.	When relieved
8th CANADIAN FIELD AMBULANCE. 2 Sections.	HAUTE AVESNES	Evening of Oct.23rd 1918.	Whole of 2/6th Lon Fd. Ambulance.	New area	Morning of Oct.24th 1918.
9th CANADIAN FIELD AMBULANCE 2 Sections	ECOIVRES	Evening of Oct.23rd 1918	Whole of 2/4th Lon Fd. ambulance	New area	Morning of Oct.24th 1918
10th CANADIAN FIELD AMBULANCE 2 Sections.	HAUTE AVESNES	Evening of Oct.23rd 1918	Whole of 2/5th Lon Fd. ambulance.	New area	Morning of Oct.24th 1918.

H.Q. 60th Division.
October 22nd 1918

A.D.M.S. 60th (London) Division.
Colonel.

Table "D".

LE CAUROY. ... ... Div. H.Q.

179th Bde. Area.   Troops.

SIBIVILLE ... Bde. H.Q.)
BUNEVILLE   ) 179th Inf. Bde.
MONTS EN TERNOIS.   ) 2/4 Fd. Co. R.E.
MONCHEAUX   ) 2/4th Fd. Amb.
SERICOURT   ) Det. Train.
HONVAL.   )

REBREUVE is added to this area for the night of the 28/29th.

180th Bde. Area.   Troops.

HOUVIN. ... Bde. H.Q.) 180th Inf. Bde.
HOUVIGNEUL   ) 1/6th Fd. Co. R.E.
CANETTEMONT.   ) 2/5th Fd. Amb.
MAGNICOURT.   ) Det. Train.

REBREUVIETTE, ROZIERE and BROUILLY are added to this area for the night of the 28/29th.

181st Bde. Area.   Troops.

BERLENCOURT ... Bde. H.Q.) 181st Inf. Bde.
MAIZIERES.   ) 3/3rd Fd. Co. R.E.
SARS LES BOIS.   ) 2/6th Fd. Amb.
DENIER.   ) Det. Train.
GOUY EN TERNOIS.   )

ETREE-WAMIN is added to this area for the night of the 28/29th.

LIENCOURT ... ... 1/12 L.N. Lancs. R.

GRAND BOURET ... ... 60 Div. Supply Column.
                     60 Mob. Vet. Sec.

WAMIN ... ... 60 Div. Train.

LE CAUROY ... ... 60 Sani: Sec.

SUBJECT:- Field Ambulance Stores.

APPENDIX III   Secret.

To. Officer Commanding,
   2/ th London Field Ambulance.

Copy

Attention is drawn to the following in addition to the instructions in H.Q. memo. C/371 of 19th inst. when Units move to New Area.

1. **Blankets.**

Mobilization Store Blankets	- Will be taken.
Blankets drawn in accordance with G.R.O. 419 (Page 42, Part II).	- Will be taken.
Blankets for personnel.	- Moved under Divl. arrangements.

   All other blankets to be handed over to incoming Unit.

2. **Hospital Clothing.**

   All Mobilization Store Clothing will be taken.

   All Clothing drawn in accordance with G.R.O. 419 will be taken.

   Other surplus Hospital Clothing will be handed over to incoming Unit.

3. **Stretchers.**

   Each Field Ambulance will hand over 50 stretchers to the incoming Unit.

4. **Stoves.**

   All surplus to Mobilization Store Table will be handed over to incoming Unit, with exception of one or more Soyer's Stoves, if found convenient to convey them later.

5. **Gas Cylinders.**

   All gas cylinders will be handed over to incoming Unit.

6. **Drugs and Dressings.**

   All surplus drugs and dressings inconvenient to carry will be handed over to incoming Unit. The Reserve Dressings at NEUVILLE ST.VAAST and MAROEUIL will be handed over to respective incoming Units, and reasons for them explained.

7. **Splints.**

   A few splints will be taken, and the remainder handed over to the incoming Unit.

8. **Red Cross Stores.**

   All Red Cross Stores will be handed over to incoming Unit.

9. **Built structures.**

   No built structures are to be dismantled.

10. **Sign Boards and Posts and Flags.**

    All these are to be taken, except large Board at AUX RIETZ.

11. **Stretcher Carriers.**

    All wheeled stretcher carriers will be taken and will be wheeled along the road with the Unit. They can be utilised for the carriage of light articles if necessary.

H.Q. 60th Div.
22-10-16.

(Sd) E.B. DOWSETT. Colonel.
A.D.M.S. 60th (London) Division.

SUBJECT:- Move.   SECRET.

MEDICAL OFFICER,
   2/ Battn. London Regiment.
----

1.   On evening of 22nd inst. an Ambulance Wagon will report to your Wagon Lines and remain there till your Unit moves, and will be entirely at your disposal for conveying sick on line of march. It should march some distance in rear of Battalion. No man is to be picked up unless he has a signed chit from you.

   You are to give the driver and wagon orderly instructions accordingly, detailing the line of route.

   The wagon is to return to its own Unit on arrival of the Battalion in its new area.

   On first day's march, all sick will be sent to HAUTE AVESNES.

   On second day's march and subsequently all sick will be sent to the Field Ambulance in your new area.

2.   <u>All</u> Stretchers and acetylene lamps are to be brought away from the trenches with the Unit.

3.   Surplus drugs and dressings may be handed over if convenient.

                              (Sd)   E. B. DOWSETT. Colonel.
H.Q. 60th Division.   A.D.M.S. 60th (London) Division.
October 22nd 1916.

Confidential.

War Diary (Medical)
of the
A.D.M.S. 60th (London) Division.
Volume.

From 1st November '16 to 30th November '16

[signature]
A.D.M.S. 60th London Div.

COMMITTEE FOR THE
MEDICAL HISTORY OF THE WAR
Date 30 APR 1917

140/949

Army Form C. 2118.

MEDICAL

WAR DIARY
or
INTELLIGENCE SUMMARY.
(Erase heading not required.)

Instructions regarding War Diaries and Intelligence Summaries are contained in F. S. Regs., Part II. and the Staff Manual respectively. Title pages will be prepared in manuscript.

Place	Date	Hour	Summary of Events and Information	Remarks and references to Appendices
BERNAVILLE	Nov 1.		To inspect medical arrangements of 1/4 London Field Ambulance at PROUVILLE and to give instructions re evacuation of sick on line of march - Inspected personnel replies to clothing and boots	A.m.D
"	Nov 2		Inspected personnel of 1/5 London Field Ambulance at LE MEILLARD and of 1/6 London Field Ambulance at HEM PLUISIR – full report re clothing & boots	A.m.D
			Operation orders L.P 7 & 9 received	
"	Nov 3	9.0 am	60th RAMC OPERATION ORDER No 5 issued	A.m.D Appendix 1
			60/15 Division H.Q. moved to AILLY LE HAUT CLOCHER.	
AILLY LE HAUT CLOCHER		12 noon	Office opened	
			2/4 London Field Ambulance moved to EAUCOURT - Reception Hospital opened	
			2/5 " " " " " BUSSUS BUSSUE - Reception Hospital opened	
			2/6 " " " " " GORGES.	
		2-30 pm	To inspect medical arrangements of 2/4 L. Field Ambulance at EAUCOURT	
			Do " " " of 2/5 L. Field Ambulance at BUSSUS BUSSUE	A.m.D
	Nov 4	2-30 pm	To see ADMS XV Corps	
"			2/1st London Field Ambulance moved to VAUCHELLES LES DOMART.	A.m.D

T2134. Wt. W708—776. 500000. 4/15. Sir J. C. & S.

Army Form C. 2118.

WAR DIARY
INTELLIGENCE SUMMARY.
(Erase heading not required.)

Place	Date	Hour	Summary of Events and Information	Remarks and references to Appendices
AILLY LE HAUT CLOCHER	Nov 5	10 am	To inspect medical arrangements of 2/5 London Field Ambulance at BUSSUS BUSSUÉ	C.in S.
"	Nov 6	11 am	To inspect medical arrangements of 2/4 London Field Ambulance at EDUCOURT.	
		2 p.m.	To AMIENS. To make arrangements for Dental and Eye treatment. Arrangements made with No 2 Stationary Hospital for such cases as may require further	
		3.30pm	DDMS IV Army visited office with regard to personnel.	C.in S.
"	Nov 7	12 noon	To inspect medical arrangements of 2/5 London Field Ambulance at BUSSUS BUSSUÉ.	
		2 pm	To see DDMS XV Corps - Then to inspect medical arrangements of 2/4 London Field Ambulance at EDUCOURT.	C.in S.
"	Nov 8	10.15am	To 2/4 London Field Ambulance at EDUCOURT with regard to increasing accommodation	
		2.15pm	MEDICAL BOARD Sat - President ADMS - Members - MAJR FEGEN DADMS and Lieut YOUNG RAMC.	C.in S.
"			In acc. orders from DMS IV" Army Lieut THOMPSON 2/5 London Field Ambulance reported for duty to ADMS XI Division and Lieut Mc DOWELL 2/5 London Field Ambulance reported for duty to ADMS 32nd Division. MEDICAL BOARD Sat - President ADMS - Members Major FEGEN DADMS and Lieut YOUNG RAMC -	C.in S.

Army Form C. 2118.

WAR DIARY
of
INTELLIGENCE SUMMARY.
(Erase heading not required.)

Instructions regarding War Diaries and Intelligence Summaries are contained in F. S. Regs., Part II. and the Staff Manual respectively. Title pages will be prepared in manuscript.

Place	Date	Hour	Summary of Events and Information	Remarks and references to Appendices
AILLY-LE-HAUT-CLOCHER	Oct 10/11	10-11pm	Lieut & R.M. W.J. TITE reported for duty with 9/4 London Field Ambulance. Capt DFA NEILSON T.C. Capt C.H. NEWTON T.C. Lieut R.H.S. MARSHALL T.C. reporting for duty and posted to 2/5th London Field Ambulance. Lieut R. CURIE T.F. reported for duty and was posted to 2/4th London Field Ambulance. Inspected medical arrangements of 2/6th London Field Ambulance in VAUCHELLES-LES-DOMART. MEDICAL BOARD under President ADMS. Members Major FEGEN DSO MS and Lieut YOUNG DSO MC. C.n.9	
" "	Oct 17		Lieut on from D.M.S. Capt HAWKS R.A.M.C - M.O. 2/13th Londn left to report for duty to ADMS 20th Division.	
" "		10 am	Lieut R. COVEN T.C. reported for duty from 20th Division – posted to Rouen with 2/1 2nd Field Ambulance. To inspect organisation of 2/4th & 2/5th London Field Ambulances and to interview new Officers.	
" "		11 am	DADMS 60th Division accompanied DADMS XV CORPS to look for site for Divisional Rest Station.	
" "		2-30pm	MEDICAL BOARD Sat - President ADMS. - Members Major FEGEN DSO MS and Lieut YOUNG RAMC. C.n.9	
" "	Mon		Lieut back in trn from DMS IV Army. Lieut V CRAMER - M.O. D.A.C left to report for duty with 20th Division. Capt Q.L. THORNTON R.A.M.C. T.C. reported for duty with 60th D.A.C.	

T2184. Wt. W708-776. 500000. 4/15. Sir J. C. & S.

Army Form C. 2118.

WAR DIARY
INTELLIGENCE SUMMARY.
(Erase heading not required.)

Place	Date	Hour	Summary of Events and Information	Remarks and references to Appendices
MOYLE HAUT CLOCHER	Nov 12th		Capt A.R. ESLER R.A.M.C. T.F. Reported for duty from 1st Division. posted to 2/5 London Field Ambulance	IV.
			Capt A.P. COMYN R.A.M.C - T.F. posted for duty with Bde. R.E.	
			Capt RF HARDCASTLE R.A.M.C. T.F. posted [joined] to 2/5th London Field Ambulance	
			Capt H.D. LEEMBRUGGEN R.A.M.C. T.F. Rejoined on return from ENGLAND and posted for duty with Pack Echelon A.S.C.	
"	Nov 13th	11 am	To inspect medical arrangements of 2/5 London Field Ambulance at BUSSUS BUSSUEL	Ch. 9
			Lieut S.M.X R.A.M.C. T.C. Reported for duty from 33rd Division posted to 2/5th London Field Ambulance	
		10 am	To inspect medical arrangement of 2/4 London Field Ambulance at ENCOURT and of 2/5 London	
			Field Ambulance at VAUCHELLES LES DOMART	
		2.30 pm	Medical Board for - Brigadier ARMS - Meandin Piatt, MT EBZEN DAVIS and	
			Capt COMYN R.A.M.C	
			Operation order No 6	Ch. F
"	Nov 14		Lieut R. GAVAN (102) R.A.M.C. T.C. reported for duty from 20th Aux. Train for duty with 2/5 London Field Ambulance	
			2/5 London Field Ambulance entrained at LONGPRE	Ch. D

Army Form C. 2118.

WAR DIARY
or
INTELLIGENCE SUMMARY.
(Erase heading not required.)

Instructions regarding War Diaries and Intelligence Summaries are contained in F. S. Regs., Part II. and the Staff Manual respectively. Title pages will be prepared in manuscript.

Place	Date	Hour	Summary of Events and Information	Remarks and references to Appendices
BILLY MONTIGNY CLOSSER	Nov 15		Goth Div: RAMC OPERATION ORDER No 6 issued. Lieut & Q.M. W.F. HILL reported for duty with 2/1st London Field Ambulance from 1st Division	Appendix II
" "	Nov 16	10.30am	To inspect arrangements of 2/1 London field Amb arrived on review	C.L.J.
" "	Nov 17	2.30pm	Conference with Senior Med O's at ADMS Office	C.L.J.
" "		11am	To inspect medical arrangements of 2/1 London Field Amb at Busses Busses and of 2/1st London Field Amb at VAUCHELLES les DOMART	
			Capt NEWTON posted to 2/1 London field Ambulance from 2/1 London Field Ambulance, vice Capt RUPROW invalided sick	
		2.30pm	Medical Board Set – President ADMS, Members Major FAGAN RAMC and Lieut YEUNG RAMC	C.L.J.
" "	Nov 18		To LILLERS to view entraining of first part 2/1/5 London field Amb. for MARSEILLES.	C.L.J.
" "	Nov 19	11am	To LONAPRE to view entraining 2nd & 3rd parts 2/1/5 London field Amb.	
		2.30pm	Medical Board sat – President ADMS Members Major FAGAN RAMC & Lieut YOUNGMAN RAMC	
			Capt D POTIVAER RAMC T.C. reported for duty from 31st Division posted to 2/5 London field Amb.	
			Capt E P BLASHKI RAMC T.C. reported for duty from 33rd Division posted to 2/5 London field Amb.	
			Under orders from DMS IV Army Capt ESLER left to rejoin 2nd Division	C.L.J.

Army Form C. 2118.

WAR DIARY
or
INTELLIGENCE SUMMARY.
(Erase heading not required.)

Instructions regarding War Diaries and Intelligence Summaries are contained in F. S. Regs., Part II. and the Staff Manual respectively. Title pages will be prepared in manuscript.

Place	Date	Hour	Summary of Events and Information	Remarks and references to Appendices
ARGYLE HAUT CLOCHER	Nov 20	10 am	To inspect 1/6 Lon. Field Ambulance at VAUCHELLES LES DOMART	C. in 7
"	Nov 21	2.2? pm	To inspect arrangements H 2/3 London Field Ambulance at VAUCHELLES LES DOMART	C. in 7
"	Nov 22	11 am	To 1/6 Lon Field Amb. at VAUCHELLES LES DOMART	C. in 7
"	"	2.30	To 101st Field Ambulance at LONGPRE - Truck arrangements regarding sick etc.	
			Many have been established on 1/6 London Field Amb: nursing	C. in 7
	Nov 23		Office routine. Sincere attn.	C. in 7
"	Nov 24	9.00 am	H.B. motor Lorries at LONGPRE - Embarked for MARSEILLES at 3.0 pm	
			15 Tents of 1/6 London Field Amb. marked.	C. in 7
"	Nov 25		In train	C. in 7
"	Nov 26		In train	C. in 7
"	Nov 27	2.30 am	Arrived MARSEILLES	C. in 7
		11-0	To see DMS BASE	
"	Nov 28	2.0 pm	To Camp at VALENTIN	C. in 7
"	Nov 29	10.00 am	To Camp at CARCASSONNE	C. in 7
"	Nov 30	10.0 am	Embarked on H.M.T. IVERNIA	C. in 7
		4 pm	H.M.T. sailed	

E. Fotheringham COLONEL
ASSISTANT DIRECTOR OF MEDICAL SERVICES

Appendix 1.

SECRET

Copy No. 10

60th DIVISION R.A.M.C. OPERATION ORDER No. 5.

Nov. 2nd 1916.

Ref. Maps.- LENS - Sheet 11. & ABBEVILLE Sheet 14 - 1 in 100,000.

1. The Division will move Westwards on 3rd November, 1916.

2. The Field Ambulances will receive their times and orders of march and destinations from the G.Os.C. Brigade Areas in which they are situated at present.

3. The Sanitary Section will move as follows:-

Starting Point	Time	Route	Destination
Road Junction S.W. end of BERNAVILLE, N. of first E in Pt. VACQUERIE.	9-50 am	RIBEAUCOURT FRANSU ERGNIES.	AILLY LE HAUT CLOCHER.

4. Divisional Headquarters will close at BERNAVILLE at 9-30 am, and open at AILLY LE HAUT CLOCHER at 11 am.

5. All sick in Field Ambulances will, as far as possible, be evacuated previous to moving.

6. Each O.C. Field Ambulance must make arrangements for the collection of sick on the line of march of the respective Brigades to which they are attached, and forward copy of the instructions to each H.O. of the Brigade, to the H.Q. of Brigade, and to the A.D.M.S.

7. Acknowledge.

E R Dawson
Colonel
A.D.M.S. 60th (London) Division.

Copy No. 1 2/4th Lon. Fd. Amb.
       2 2/5th   "
       3 2/6th   "
       4 60th Lon. Sanitary Sect.
       5 Headquarters, 60th Division.
       6 179th Infantry Brigade.
       7 180th   "
       8 181st   "
       9 File
      10 War Diary
      11 Duplicate War Diary.

Appendix II

SECRET.   Copy No. 6

60th DIVISION R.A.M.C. OPERATION ORDER NO. 6.

November 13th 1916.

Reference Maps.
   LENS Sheet 11 and ABBEVILLE Sheet 14 & AMIENS Sheet 17
   all 1 in 100,000.

1. The Division will move to entraining Station at LONGPRÉ commencing on November 14th 1916.

2. The 2/4th London Field Ambulance will move as follows:-

STARTING POINT.	TIME OF PASSING S.P.	ROUTE.
Cross Roads HAUCOURT SUR SOMME.	11-40 am	PONT REMY. LIERCOURT. FONTAINE.

3. Other Medical Units of Division will remain in their present billets until further orders.

4. 2/4th London Field Ambulance will evacuate all sick before starting, and will send Motor Ambulance Cars at present with that Unit to report to A.D.M.S. Office.

5. Acknowledge.

                                                              Colonel.
                                              A.D.M.S. 60th (London) Division.

Issued at 6 pm.

Copy No. 1. 2/4th F.A.
        2. 2/5th F.A.
        3. 2/6th F.A.
        4. 60th Div. Sanitary Section.
        5. 60th Div. H.Q.
        6. War Diary.
        7. Duplicate War Diary.
        8. File.

www.ingramcontent.com/pod-product-compliance
Lightning Source LLC
Chambersburg PA
CBHW081449160426
43193CB00013B/2419